GREAT
TURNING
POINTS
IN HISTORY

Van Nostrand Reinhold Company Regional Offices:
New York Cincinnati Chicago Millbrae Dallas

Van Nostrand Reinhold Company International Offices:
London Toronto Melbourne

Copyright © 1971 by Louis L. Snyder

Library of Congress Catalog Card Number 71-143186

Published by Van Nostrand Reinhold Company,
a Division of Litton Educational Publishing, Inc.,
450 West 33rd Street, New York, N.Y. 10001

Published simultaneously in Canada by
Van Nostrand Reinhold Company Ltd.

16 15 14 13 12 11 10 9 8 7 6 5 4 3 2 1

GREAT TURNING POINTS IN HISTORY

Louis L. Snyder

VNR Van Nostrand Reinhold Company

NEW YORK   CINCINNATI   TORONTO   LONDON   MELBOURNE

TO
FAYE LIEBERMAN

CONTENTS

Introduction   1

Battle of Marathon   5

Crucifixion of Jesus   10

Flight of Muhammad from Mecca to Medina, 622 A.D.   15

Battle of Tours, 732 A.D.   20

Coronation of Charlemagne, 800 A.D.   26

Crusades: The Speech of Urban II, 1095   30

Magna Carta, 1215   37

The Invention of Printing, c. 1445   42

Discovery of America by Christopher Columbus, 1492   48

Luther Before the Diet of Worms, 1521   58

The Spanish Armada, 1588   66

Rout of the Turks at Vienna, 1683   74

Newton's *Principia* Revolutionizes the Scientific World, 1687   78

Fall of the Bastille, 1789   85

Napoleon's Retreat from Moscow, 1812   91

The Communist Manifesto, 1847–48   98

The Opening of Japan, 1853   103

Africa: Stanley Meets Livingstone, 1871   111

Flight of the Wright Brothers at Kitty Hawk, 1903   118

Assassination at Sarajevo, June 28, 1914   123

Sinking of the *Lusitania*, May 7, 1915   129

Storming of the Winter Palace, November 7, 1917   137

Battle of Britain, 1940   145

Epic of Stalingrad, 1942   152

Atomic Bomb Dropped on Hiroshima, August 6, 1945   157

INTRODUCTION

A MATTER OF DEFINITION

THE CASCADING waters of the Colorado River rush on to a given point where there is a 90-degree turn. Here the river spreads out, temporarily loses its rage, and meanders on peacefully for several miles, only to strike another narrow gorge which increases its velocity. This pattern of natural phenomenon has its counterpart in the course of historical development. There are many turning points in the history of man from Adam to atom, from *Pithecanthrophus erectus* to Charles de Gaulle.

A turning point in history is an event, happening, or stage which thrusts the course of historical development into a different direction. By definition a turning point is a great event, but it is even more − a great event with the explosive impact of altering the trend of man's life on this planet.

As a matter of convenience, turning points may be divided into major and minor varieties. There are literally thousands of minor turning points, many of them limited to matters of national importance, for both small and large nations. The flight of Rudolf Hess to England on May 10, 1941, was a minor turning point in the history of Nazism because it signaled the bankruptcy of Hitler's insane Third Reich. But the battle of Stalingrad was a major turning point in the history of the twentieth century because it smashed the pretensions of Nazi Germany. Visualize a world of concentration camps, which would have been an even greater catastrophe than the current combination of competing selfish national states.

This book is concerned exclusively with the big ones − those major turning points which sent the mainstream of history tumbling in a new direction. It seeks in summary narrative to re-create those awesome events which most historians would be inclined to accept as key hinges of historical change. At the same time it tries to avoid the quicksand of complicated historical analysis.

LACK OF SCIENTIFIC PATTERN

There is no discernible pattern in the appearance of historical turning points. The reason is that history is not and never was a pure science. Science is based on the immovability and immutability of nature, upon natural laws which are regular and quantitative and which can be ascertained through statistics. What the scientist lacks in evidence can have no effect upon the physical universe. The physicist, the chemist, the geologist, the botanist, the astronomer — all the pure scientists — deal with facts from which they can draw accurate generalizations and laws.

How different is the vast domain of the historian! His world exists only in what is recorded directly or by inference. He is faced with overwhelming unknowns. Thomas Edison is supposed to have remarked that we know only one millionth of one per cent of what is to be known; to that judgment every historian is willing to add a fervent "Amen." There is a vast multitude of phenomena in the course of historical development — peoples, personalities, conditions, and happenings. "The world of human happenings," says Erich Kahler, "appears to be an inexhaustible wealth of motley, chaotic, peculiar, and chance-propelled entities."

All this is in contrast with the domain of scientific research. Unlike the scientist, the historian does not have the advantage of experimentation and quantification — he is faced with a huge variety of complexities which are difficult to place in meaningful categories. There are too many unknowns to set up "historical laws." Where science is concerned with the general, history deals with the individual and the particular. Therefore, historians find it best to limit their generalizations when speaking of events and institutions.

This is not to say that historians shrink from battle. They will be ready at the drop of a footnote to make generalizations about the past and hint that the future will certainly fall within the patterns of pat formulae. This has become, in fact, a recognized pursuit among historians, and often the stature of a historian is measured by the elaborateness of a thesis into which he fits all the variegated developments of the past.

We see this tendency in Marx's historical materialism and its class struggle, surplus value, internationalism, and inevitability theses. We see it in Buckle's theory of climate in history, Carlyle's great-man concept, Spengler's seasonal cycle of spring-summer-fall-winter in the rise and decline of civilizations, and Toynbee's challenge-and-response in the creation of cultures. We see it in Turner's frontier thesis, Mahan's theory of the influence of sea power, Pirenne on medieval urbanization, Sombart and Tawney on the rise of capitalism, and Troeltsch and Renan on hypotheses of religious change.

All these scholars seek to explain the "actual" historical universe and attempt to project concepts which will be acceptable generally to all historians. It is neither presumptuous nor incorrect to say that none of these shining lights has succeeded in his gigantic task. The vast expanse of historical development remains mysterious and incomprehensible. In the scientific world, Newton was able to build on the contributions of Copernicus, Kepler, and Galileo to construct his synthesis of gravitation. Thus far no comparable historian has appeared to clarify "historical laws," though certainly the efforts of Marx, Spengler, Toynbee, and the rest should be given a gold (or red) star for a good try at an impossible task.

PREDICTING TURNING POINTS

History is concerned with the past. It is difficult enough for historians to find generalizations about past events and institutions. There are far too many un-knowns to enable accurate prediction about what is going to happen in the future. Careful historians, says Louis Gottschalk, ought to limit themselves to stressing one among several possible outcomes when a current variation appears to be analogous to a past one.

Karl Marx called attention to the importance of economic factors in history, but the predictive qualities of his inevitability thesis have won him few laurels. He prophesied that the economic revolution would come to highly industrialized Britain or Germany, but instead it had its first stage in agricultural, almost feudal Russia. The prediction was inaccurate.

In the words of Edward H. Carr, "Nothing in history is inevitable except in the formal sense that, for it to happen otherwise, the antecedent causes would have to be different." There are always multitudes of causes, interrelated and interacting, and few of them can be isolated. It is a difficult enough task to make sense out of the complex coherence of the past without using crystal balls to divine the future.

Turning points in history may appear at any time and at any place. They may not seem important at the time. The assassination at Sarajevo on June 28, 1914, was the spark that kindled World War I. Yet, this critical event found no place on the front page of *The New York Times*: the immediate reaction was that it was another of those interminable, insignificant, and unpronounceable Balkan plots. Historians might have had a vague idea that the combination of imperialism, nationalism, militarism, and international anarchy was leading straight to worldwide conflict, but they had no idea as to where or when it would explode.

A PLEA FOR TEMPORARY SUBJECTIVITY

The great historian Leopold von Ranke urged his colleagues to complete objectivity — merely to tell what happened — *"wie es eigentlich gewesen ist."* For generations these words have been taken to heart by American scholars anxious to look at history without bias. In his pre-Freudian milieu, Ranke never realized the unconscious motivations which made his ideal of pure objectivity an unattainable dream. In the very process of selecting his "facts" the historian reveals or betrays innermost prejudices. The truly "objective" historian stands in danger of becoming a mere chronicler or annalist. The instant he seeks causation or interpretation he sacrifices his impartiality.

All this by way of apprising the reader that these twenty-five major turning points in history are not presented as *the* most important ones of all time. They represent merely the selections of one observer and are conditioned by his own motivations. Another historian might agree on a majority of the titles, still another on only a few of them. One man's choice may be another man's rejection. An attempt will be made in each case to present reasons for the selection, without going into interminable argument with footnotes heckling the text in order to prove the wisdom of each choice.

The reader will undoubtedly have his own nominations for inclusion in the category of major turning points. He may well find some of them in this collection. Good hunting and pleasant subjective reminiscences of the history classroom!

Many thanks to my wife, who as always has spent many hours and days on this project and has given it the benefit of her editorial ability and good judgment.

— Louis L. Snyder

BATTLE OF MARATHON, 490 B.C.[1]

*"Until that time the very name of Medes
had been a terror for the Greeks to hear."*

THE EYE of ancient historians can find dozens of turning points in the history of
the early Egyptians and Mesopotamians. The invasion of Egypt by the Hyksos and
the display of Hammurabi's Code in Babylonia would certainly be included among
the more important hinges of change. But for our first attention let us omit the
ancient cradlelands and consider the battle of Marathon in 490 B.C., as a result of
which civilization moved westward instead of toward the Near Orient. At this point
the westward expansion of the Persians was halted, and Western civilization took on
its Greek complexion.

In the words of the historian C. A. Robinson, "It was now demonstrated that
the Greek warrior was superior to the Persian. . . . The Greeks were inspired with a
fair hope of maintaining their freedom. To the Athenians, who almost singlehanded
had beaten a power thought to be irresistible, this victory served as an incentive to
heroism. The glory of the Marathonian warriors never faded."

The topography of ancient Greece made for political disunity, but there were
several unifying factors in Greek life, such as the use of a common language, similar
religious and cultural characteristics, and a desire for expansion. Greek colonial
expansion was rapid. Between 750 and 55 B.C., Greek cities appeared in all sections
of the Mediterranean area. The basic motive for expansion was economic. As the
population increased the Greeks found their sparse land too poor to support them
and as a remedy began to search for new fertile areas. Added to this was a desire for

---

[1] The date generally given is 490 B.C., but the *Cambridge Ancient History*, iv, 245, has
"probably the 21st September, 491 B.C."

increased trade and industry, for new markets, and for sources of raw materials. Political motives included the imperial ambitions of city-states and the efforts of ostracized political leaders to find new habitats. Greek imperialists followed the line of least resistance — they were blocked to the east by the powerful Persian Empire. It was a classic confrontation that was to be repeated many times in subsequent historical development.

A clash between the two expanding imperialisms, Greek and Persian, started after Ionian Greek cities on the coast of Asia Minor revolted, from 499 to 494 B.C., against the rule of Persian King Darius. Then the most powerful city in Greece, Athens sent twenty warships to the Greek cities in Asia Minor. But the revolt was crushed by Darius, who was determined to destroy Athens and maintain the unity of his empire.

In 490 B.C., another Persian expedition set out from Asia Minor across the Aegean Sea to the Bay of Marathon. Together with their allies, the Medes, the Persian invaders numbered about 20,000 men. The force was commanded by Datis, a Mede, and Artaphernes, a nephew of Darius. Along the route most of the islanders submitted at once. The Persians aimed to smash Eretria and Athens, and bring their peoples as slaves before the Great King.

Eretria, besieged for six days, was betrayed by two of her citizens. The city was sacked and the population taken into captivity. The angry Athenians were unwilling to expose their city by sending a force to help Eretria. Instead, they sent Pheidippides, a professional long-distance runner and Olympic champion, to Sparta to request help. For two days and two nights he traveled, swimming rivers and climbing mountains. But the Spartans, in the midst of a festival, replied that they could not possibly send assistance until the moon was full. Meanwhile, the Persian host, guided by the aged Hippias, former tyrant of Athens, turned to the task of destroying Eretria. Persians and Medes landed at Marathon "thinking to do the same to the Athenians."

Marathon was a plain about five miles long by two miles wide on the east coast of Attica just 24 miles northeast of Athens. There was a large marsh at its northern end, a smaller one to the south. The Athenians took position in a narrow valley at Vrana facing the Persians, who were on the plain adjoining the shore. There were 9,000 Athenians and 1,000 Plataean heavy infantry, a total of 10,000 men, against a force at least twice as large. A council of war, consisting of ten generals, decided to give final command to Miltiades, who had special knowledge of the Persians.

There were two opinions among the Athenian generals. Some, wanting to avoid battle, said that there were too few Athenians to engage the invaders. Others, Miltiades among them, were for fighting. Miltiades went up to the Polemarch (military commander) and said: "It lies with you, Callimachus, to enslave Athens or make her free, and in making her free to leave a memory behind you so long as there are men alive . . . . There are ten of us generals, and we are equally divided: some would have us fight and some would not . . . . If we do go into battle before any rot sets in among the Athenians, given equal favor of the gods, it is in our power to conquer . . . . If you decide with me, behold your country free and the city the foremost in Greece. But if you choose the opinion of those who would by all means prevent us from fighting, your lot will be the reverse of those blessings."

With these passionate words Miltiades won Callimachus over to his side. The Polemarch's vote tipped the scale in favor of resistance.

What we know of the battle of Marathon we owe to the Greek historian Herodotus (c.484-425 B.C.), called the "Father of History." The son of Lyxos and Dryo, he was born at Halicarnassus in Caria, then a Persian dependency, probably six years after the battle at Marathon had taken place. As a young man he began reading on a vast scale. During the years 464-454 B.C., he traveled extensively in Greece and the Mediterranean area, including the Near East, collecting a vast amount of geographical, ethnographical, and archaeological information for his great *History*. About 447 B.C. he settled at Athens, but finding it impossible to obtain a vote, he sailed in 444 together with a party of colonists for Magna Graecia in southern Italy, where he spent the remainder of his days.

Herodotus's *History* was completed in 445 B.C. It is said that he was given the sum of 10 talents as a reward for his work. The early books describe the rise and development of the kingdoms of Greece and Persia. The battle of Marathon is recounted in Book VI. The style is attractive, written primarily for recitation.

The description by Herodotus is concise and to the point. The Athenian right wing was led by Callimachus, for it was the Athenian custom to give the Polemarch command of the right of the line. Beginning from the right, the tribes were ranged one after another. At the end were the Plataeans, responsible for the left wing. The line was weak in the center, but both wings were strong. Herodotus remarked that after the battle, when the Athenians offered their sacrifices in the congregations at the four-yearly festivals, they would pray for the good of Athenians and Plataeans alike.

As soon as the omens proved favorable, the Athenians, given the word, advanced on the invaders. The distance between the armies was about eight furlongs. Seeing the Athenians approach, the Persians made ready for resistance. Obviously, these mad Athenians were as good as lost, being so few and thrusting forth at so great a pace, without the benefit of either horsemen or archers.

Herodotus described it in a famous passage:

> So when the battle was set in array, and the victims showed themselves favorable, instantly the Athenians ... charged the barbarians at a run. Now the distance between the two armies was a little short of a mile. The Persians, therefore, when they saw the Greeks coming on at speed, made ready to receive them, although it seemed to them that the Athenians were bereft of their senses, and bent upon their own destruction; for they saw a mere handful of men coming on at a run without either horsemen or archers .... The Athenians in close array fell upon them, and fought in a manner worthy of being recorded. They were the first of the Greeks, so far as I know, who introduced the custom of charging the enemy at a run, and they were likewise the first who dared to look upon the Median garb, and to face men clad in that fashion. Until that time the very name of the Medes had been a terror to the Greeks to hear.

For a time the center of the Greek line was in trouble. At first the Persians got the better of the Greeks, broke their line, and forced them inland. But on the wings the Athenians and the Plataeans were victorious. Both wings closed in on the Persians who had broken through the center. The invaders fled, pursued by the Greeks, who went after them and hewed them down until they came to the shore.

At this point Callimachus, after distinguishing himself, lost his life. Other Greek leaders were also slain. Cynaegirus, the son of Euphorion, seized an enemy vessel by the ornament at the stern, only to have his hand cut off by the blow of an axe.

The Greeks took seven enemy ships. But the Persians managed to board the rest and moved away from the shore, taking with them their Eretrian prisoners. They set off for Athens, hoping to reach the city before the Greeks could get there by land. But the Athenians ran fast to the rescue of the city, and got there first. The Persian fleet soon arrived, and stayed off the nearby port for a while. But after resting on their oars, the invaders departed and sailed toward home.

The Persians lost about 6,400 men in the battle, the Athenians 192. Herodotus related a marvelous happening in the midst of the battle. One of the Athenians, Epizelus, son of Cyphagoras, while fighting courageously in the thick of combat, was suddenly stricken blind. He lost the sight of both eyes even though he was not hit in any part of his body and remained blind for the rest of his life. "And I heard that he gave an account of what befell him: he said that a gigantic warrior, with a huge beard that shaded his shield, stood over against him. The apparition passed him by, and killed the man next to him. Such, as I understand it, was the tale which Epizelus told."

The description of Marathon by Herodotus has satisfied few historians. Admitting that it is a graphic sketch, they complain that it is wanting in accuracy of detail, and that it fails to give minute allusions to localities which alone could enable the reader to reproduce in imagination the struggle as it actually occurred. Herodotus failed to note the exact numbers engaged on either side; he neglected to mark the position of either army; he did not describe the disposition which the Greek leaders made of their troops; and he paid no attention to the tactics of the Persian commanders. Worst of all, he was silent on the subject of the Persian cavalry, forgetting to tell what part it took in the action, nor offering any explanation of its apparent absence.

Herodotus did not give any satisfactory account of why both sides delayed so long before the battle. He did not explain why Miltiades decided to strike when he did. Why did the Persian center break and pursue the Greeks into the inner country? Why the smallness of the Greek loss, incompatible with such a rout? What became of the Persian cavalry? Almost certainly messengers must have been sent to call for the cavalry as soon as combat began, but according to Herodotus, the horsemen did not arrive until the battle was over. Perhaps they made their appearance before nightfall and were able to re-embark quietly, for the Greeks could not have been anxious for a second encounter.

Herodotus probably learned about the battle from the sons and grandsons of those who took part in the battle. He was weak on both chronology and military operations: he seemed unable to think out a strategical combination or a tactical movement. Yet, we have no better account of the famous battle.

Marathon took on tremendous significance — perhaps even exaggerated — in the Greek mind. Mighty Persia, symbol of strength in her contemporary world, had been defeated by a tiny, almost insignificant Greek city-state. Athens emerged from obscurity to first-rate power. The Greek hoplite — the heavy-armed infantry soldier — had demonstrated his superiority on the battlefield. Athens became aware of her new strength and began to overestimate it.

True, the westward advance of Persia was halted in this crucial battle, but this was by no means the end of the Persian Wars. Darius died without having avenged himself upon the Greeks. His son, Xerxes, determined to finish his father's task, gathered a huge army from all sections of his empire and built a powerful navy. The Greek city-states, meanwhile, having by this time learned the value of cooperation, organized to meet the Persians. An army of 200,000 Persians[2] was met at Thermopylae in 480 B.C. by a Greek force of 7,300 men under command of a Spartan, Leonidas. After a stubborn defense, the Greeks were annihilated. The Persians entered Athens and leveled the city. But at the naval battle of Salamis, the Persians were almost wiped out. On the same day, a Greek force routed the Carthaginian allies of Persia. In 479 B.C. another Persian force was destroyed at Plataea. The Persians were driven out of the continent by 466 B.C., and they never again set foot upon Europe.

The Persian Wars resulted in the triumph of Greek civilization over the Oriental, in the development of Greek unity, and in the spread throughout Western Europe of the free Greek spirit as opposed to Oriental authoritarianism. This was truly a major turning point in the history of civilization.

For the Greeks the glory of the Marathonian warriors never faded. The Greek poet Aeschylus, as his epitaph noted, wanted to be remembered not by his magnificent dramas, but by his role in the battle of Marathon:

> This tomb the dust of Aeschylus doth hide —
> Euphorion's son and fruitful Gela's pride;
> How famed his valor Marathon may tell, —
> And long-haired Medes, who knew it all too well.

---

[2] Herodotus wildly exaggerated the number as more than five millions, including noncombatants, and 1,207 warships. A reasonable estimate would be 200,000 combatants and 700 warships.

CRUCIFIXION OF JESUS

"He was clearly a person — to use a common phrase — of intense personal magnetism."

AMONG the more important hinges of history was the growth of Christianity in the late days of the Roman Empire. The once brilliant civilization was in decline. Always weak in creative genius, Rome came to depend upon the formulas of the past and upon imitations of the incomparably greater culture of the Greeks. The citizenry, possessing no satisfactory philosophy of life, faced a moral collapse. The Roman mind became lazy and doubly uncreative until it was unable to withstand the inroads of the culturally inferior barbarians. The edifice of Roman culture, old and decrepit, was on the verge of tumbling down.

From the early days of the Republic to the Empire, the average Roman looked upon the idea of citizenship as a privilege and obligation, for he was confident of his rights under the law and he was willing to make sacrifices for his country. But the growth of slavery and the general breakdown of social life tended to undermine his faith in his once precious citizenship.

Both aristocracy and masses were infected by weak morale. The patrician class, losing its sense of family life, failed to support the state that had granted it many privileges. The masses, without wealth, began to lose interest in service to the state, gradually withdrew from the professions of politics, army, law, and bureaucracy, and finally lost all desire to uphold and extend the power of the state.

Disintegration of the body politic set in under the influence of this mentality. Men who once rushed to the defense of Rome in critical times now refused to serve her in the armies. Others, disgusted with conditions of life, refused to raise families. While the whole fabric of Roman society was in process of decomposition, the Germanic barbarians, to whom the Romans had carried their civilization, began to infiltrate into the empire. At first received as welcome settlers, the barbarians were later enrolled in the Roman armies. They began to revolt against their benefactors, and finally attained the upper hand. Weakened by economic and political dry rot, by increasing wealth on the one hand and misery on the other, and by mental and moral ossification, the Romans became easy prey for the invaders.

To this declining Roman society, Jesus would offer a novel and vital spirit, an emotional outlet to the wealthy, and salvation in the next world for the common man. His doctrines of love, peace, tolerance, and justice were attractive to a jaded and unhappy people.

During the second triumvirate of Octavian, Antony, and Lepidus (43-28 B.C.), a Judean poet in Egypt foretold the destruction of the entire heathen world and the dawn of the Kingdom of God, in which a holy king — the Messiah (from the Hebrew *Mashiach*, "The Anointed One") — would hold the scepter. The Messiah would reestablish the independence of the Jews, make Jerusalem the spiritual kingdom of the world, resurrect the dead, and bring forth a new heaven and a new earth. "When Rome shall vanquish Egypt and govern her, then shall the greatest in the kingdom, the immortal King, arise in the world, and a holy King will come to rule over all the nations of the earth during all time." In Judea, radical religious sects kept the people in ferment as one mystic after another claimed to be the Messiah. All agreed that he must spring from the house of David.

John the Baptist sent out the cry: "The Messiah is coming! The Kingdom of Heaven is near!" He invited all to come and receive baptism in the Jordan, to confess and renounce their sins, and thereby to prepare for the advent of the Kingdom of Heaven.

While Caesar Augustus, first of the Roman emperors, was reigning in Rome, Jesus was born in Bethlehem, a city in Judea, probably in the fourth year (or perhaps the sixth) before the Christian era. The birth was recorded in the Gospels of St. Luke and St. Matthew:

> And it came to pass in those days, that there went out a decree from Caesar Augustus, that all the world should be taxed. And all went to be taxed, every one into his own city.
>
> And Joseph also went up from Galilee, out of the city of Nazareth, into Judea, unto the city of David, which is called Bethlehem; (because he was of the house and lineage of David:) to be taxed with Mary his espoused wife, being great with child.
>
> And so it was, that, while they were there, the days were accomplished that she should be delivered. And she brought forth her firstborn son, and wrapped him in swaddling clothes, and laid him in a manger; because there was no room for them in the inn.

Little is known of the early life of Jesus before the age of thirty. He appeared in Judea as a teacher, like other Jewish prophets who wandered about the country-side. From the four Gospels appears a being of passionate zeal, who preached an exciting doctrine of the universal loving Fatherhood of God and the coming of the Kingdom of Heaven. Unconventional, Jesus feasted with sinners, forgave an adulteress, healed the sick, and preached a doctrine of love, peace, and good will. The doctrine of the Kingdom of God advocated a revolutionary economic philosophy that struck hard at the roots of the Roman state, the Roman religion, and Judaism. Denouncing private wealth on the ground that all men and all possessions belonged to the Kingdom of God, Jesus exhorted all those who were heavily laden to come and find rest. He preached against class privilege and wealth, warning that rich men would not enter the Kingdom of God unless they disposed of their property first and gave it to the poor:

> And Jesus looked round about, and saith unto his disciples, "How hardly shall they that have riches enter into the Kingdom of God." And the disciples were astonished at his words. But Jesus answereth again, and saith unto them, "Children, how hard it is for them that trust in riches to enter into the Kingdom of God. It is easier for a camel to go through the eye of a needle, than for a rich man to enter into the Kingdom of God."

Millions of words have been written about the life of Jesus, but few word-portraits can match this extraordinary picture by H. G. Wells: [1]

> But just as the personality of Gautama Buddha has been distorted and obscured by the stiff squatting figure, the gilded idol of later Buddhism, so one feels that the lean and strenuous personality of Jesus is much wronged by the unreality and conventionality that a mistaken reverence has imposed upon his figure in modern Christian art. Jesus was a penniless teacher, who wandered about the dusty sun-lit country of Judea, living upon casual gifts of food; yet he is always represented clean, combed, and sleek, in spotless raiment, erect, and with something motionless about him as though he were gliding through the air. This alone has made him unreal and incredible to many people who cannot distinguish the core of the story from the ornamental and unwise additions of the unintelligently devout.
>
> We are left, if we do strip this record of these difficult accessories, with the figure of a being, very human, very earnest and passionate, capable of swift anger, and teaching a new and simple and profound doctrine — namely, the universal loving Fatherhood of God and the coming of the Kingdom of Heaven. He was clearly a person — to use a common phrase — of intense personal magnetism. He attracted followers and filled them with love and courage. Weak and ailing people were heartened and healed by his presence. Yet he was probably of a delicate physique, because of the swiftness with which he died under the pains of crucifixion. There is a tradition that he fainted when, according to the custom, he was made to bear his cross to the place of execution. When he first appeared as a teacher he was a man of about thirty. He went about the country

---

[1] H. G. Wells, *Outline of History* (Garden City, New York, 1949), pp. 528-529. Courtesy of Garden City Publishing Co., Inc.

for some time spreading his doctrine, and then he came to Jerusalem and was accused of trying to set up a strange kingdom in Judea; he was tried upon this charge, and crucified together with two thieves. Long before these two were dead, his sufferings were over.

For the Jews the teachings of Jesus were dismaying. Could it be true that there were no chosen people? Was it possible that all men, no matter of what race or caste, good and sinners alike, were brothers? United in close family ties, the Jews refused to accept the idea that loyalty to family must give way to a broader attachment to the Kingdom of God. They decided that this was not the true Messiah.

The Romans, too, were alienated. What did Jesus mean by crying out against the washing of pots and cups? Roman aristocrats denounced Jesus as a revolutionary who would strip them of possessions and security. Roman soldiers, dazed by teaching they could not understand, laughed and crowned the teacher as a mock Caesar.

For three years Jesus traveled around the countryside preaching the strange doctrines. He came to Jerusalem, only to be accused of seeking to set up a kingdom to rival the Roman state. His enemies, taking note of a scene at the Temple with the money lenders, resolved on drastic measures. He was betrayed by Judas Iscariot, whose earlier love had turned to hate. Jesus was convicted of blasphemy by the ecclesiastical court of the Sanhedrin, and Pontius Pilate, Roman procurator of Judea, who alone had the power, ordered the execution. The accused was forced to bear a cross to the place of execution at Golgatha. There, between two condemned thieves, Jesus was crucified in 29 or 30 A.D., at the age of thirty-four or thirty-five.

On the cross was placed a sign:

JESUS OF NAZARETH, KING OF THE JEWS

In three hours Jesus was dead, and was buried in a tomb guarded by Pilate's soldiers. In Christian belief, on the third day the crucified teacher rose again and appeared not as a ghost "but as a complete human being with a body that could walk, talk, eat, and speak." After forty days of extraordinary communion with the disciples, Jesus disappeared for the last time on the Mount of Olives, and ascended to Heaven.

The crucifixion of Jesus was a crucial turning point not only in the history of Rome but in all Western civilization. The selection of the execution itself as a turning point is an arbitrary one — either the birth or resurrection of Jesus could be substituted as the focus of change.

In the following two centuries, Christianity spread through the hollow shell of the once magnificent Roman state, and wove together a larger and larger mulititude of converts into a new politico-religious community. The expansion of Christianity supplanted a unity of political allegiance (*imperium*) by a unity of religious belief (*sacerdotium*). Overcoming early persecution by the Romans, Christianity achieved toleration, and finally became the state religion. Theodosius I forbade any Roman official in the future to hold to pagan beliefs, thereby publicly announcing the political triumph of Christianity.

Christianity was a proselytizing religion. It announced the inadequacy of all others and it was determined to convert the whole world. Paganism continued to be strong, but it gave way in Western Europe as the new religion won its way to dominance. Before the third century, Christianity was extended beyond the Empire to Persia, Armenia, Arabia, and even to the Far East. Many barbarians on the northern and western borders were Christians before the great migrations began. By 400 A.D. the Church had nearly extirpated paganism in the cities, and began the so-called evangelization of the fields.

A Christian political organization based upon that of the Roman Empire was fashioned. Early in the second century appeared the offices of bishops, presbyters, and deacons, whose duties were to administer the charities of the Church and to put an end to disorders at services. The Catholic Church was formally organized in the second century A.D. With the growth of Christian communities, a feeling of unity found expression, leading in 325 A.D. to the first general council of the Church at Nicaea. Meanwhile, the Roman episcopate was transformed into the papacy, which began to claim supremacy over the entire Christian Church. By the opening of the Middle Ages, the Church came to be regarded not only as the institution controlling salvation, but also as the ultimate political authority of the day.

Thus from humble origins, from the mind of a penniless wandering teacher, rose the great religion that was to supplant other Oriental mystery religions and in Judeo-Christian form give the West its standards of morals and ethics. With Jesus the mighty torrent of Western civilization changed its course.

FLIGHT OF MUHAMMAD FROM
MECCA TO MEDINA, 622 A.D.

*"They shall be accompanied by damsels of unsurpassed
beauty, with large black, pearl-like eyes."*

SIX hundred years after Jesus there appeared another great religion to challenge
Christianity for dominance. Islam was propelled into existence at another of
history's great turning points — the flight on camel-back of Muhammad, together
with Abu Bakr, his disciple and successor, from Mecca to Medina in 622 A.D. This
two-hundred-mile ride marked the birth of a religion for nearly a quarter of a
billion human beings in the Near East, Africa, and India.

Muhammad was about fifty-two at the time. He was born about 570 in Mecca to
a prominent family, which had charge of the *Kaaba*. This was an enclosure
containing a black stone, probably a meteorite, about as long as man's hand, and
the object of veneration and worship. Muhammad's parents died when he was
a child and he was brought up by his grandfather, after whose death he was taken
into the household of his uncle. He early became acquainted with the habits of the
Bedouins. Later he served as a caravan conductor for Meccan traders to Syria and
northern Arabia. After suffering hardships from poverty, he married a wealthy
widow, some fifteen years his senior, when he was about forty. He settled down as
a man of means, at this time a man of winning personality, of delicate health and
nervous temperament, and keenly interested in religious discussion.

At the age of twenty-five Muhammad began to have revelations in which he
heard voices speaking to him like "the reverberating of bells." Later, according to
Muhammad, the Angel Gabriel appeared to him while at prayer in a grotto on Mt.
Hira, near Mecca. When he was sleeping, a mysterious being ordered him to read or
recite. He left the cave and suddenly he heard himself called and greeted by the
name "Messenger of Allah." He looked up and saw an enormous being standing on
the horizon. Dazzled, he saw the angel gaze at him from every part of heaven.

It occurred to Muhammad that he was being chosen as a prophet by God, and that Moses and Jesus were probably his forerunners. He told his story to a small circle of friends, including his wife, Khadya; his cousin, Ali; and his friend, Abu Bakr.

He began to call men to worship one God. There were few converts – at first – only forty accepted him after four years of preaching. As long as his teaching was secret with a small number of followers, he experienced few difficulties. But with public announcement of his faith he was faced with hostility by the authorities as well as his fellow citizens, both of whom were aroused to fury by what they regarded as a new religious combination in restraint of trade. Meccan merchants decided to eliminate this presumptuous prophet.

When they heard the news, Muhammad and Abu Bakr hid in a cave for three days, and obtaining camels, they fled. A reward was offered for their capture. After seven days of hard travel across a forbidding desert of dunes, they came to the village of Quba. Several days later they entered the town which was to become Medina, the city of the Prophet. Later it was decided that the flight, the *Hegira* or *Hijra*, should become the beginning – the Year One – of the Muslim era – Friday, June 16, 622 (Julian calendar). A new era in religious history was born.

Muhammad's success in Medina marked a change in the character of the fledgling religion. Organizing an army of believers, he advanced upon Mecca and within eight years took the metropolis. Meccans adopted the religion of Islam (meaning literally "submission to the will of God") and the population became Muslims ("followers who submitted"). Muhammad now made certain not to injure the traffic to Mecca by requiring all Muslims to make the pilgrimage to the *Kaaba* as they had done when they were pagans.

Before his death in 632, Muhammad spread his word and power throughout the entire Arabian peninsula. He sent envoys to all the great rulers of the world. He married several women during his declining years, for which he was criticized by Christians. His action was defended by Arab leaders with the argument that the dozen or more wives he took in later life were all widows of his dead warriors. It was said that he had married them according to custom as a protector or to obtain an heir to succeed him.

Western critics describe Muhammad as a greedy, cunning, and hypocritical impostor. His followers judge him as the greatest holy leader of all time.

The Koran (Arabic *Qur'an* – "recitation"), the sacred book of Islam, is regarded by Muslims as the Word of God. In size it about equals the New Testament. Muslims believe that the inspired word of God existed before the Creation in the Preserved Tablet in heaven, which was communicated to Muhammad *sura* (chapter) by *sura*, verse by verse, and word by word, by the Archangel Gabriel. The Koran did not appear until shortly after Muhammad's death, when it was compiled by the order of Abu Bakr. Its contents, which were said to have been found written on palm leaves and white stones, were completed by the end of the first year after Muhammad's death. Having no scheme, plan, or chronology, it is an almost haphazard compilation of unconnected recitations dealing with many themes. No attempt is made to explain the circumstances of the delivery of the various speeches and sayings. It is probable that Muhammad learned about the old Biblical narratives from Jewish scholars. Many passages of the Koran show a direct resemblance to those of the Old Testament.

The Koran emphasizes the Oneness and Almightiness of God, as opposed to polytheism:

> He is but one God, the everlasting God who begets not, nor is begotten [obviously a reference to Jesus as the Son of God], and there is none like unto him. (*Meccan Suras, 10.*)

Muhammad is depicted as having been called first to recite the Koran and as the last and greatest of God's messengers. The Hebrew prophets and Jesus are accepted as forerunners:

> In the former times We sent Our apostles with convincing arguments and all decisive miracles, and We gave them the Scriptures. We sent to men Noah, Abraham, and the prophets, but many believed not. Then We sent Our apostles, after whom came Jesus, Son of Mary. Then, last of all, came Our great Apostle, Muhammad. O all ye believers, fear God and obey the words of Allah's messenger. (*Medina Suras, 57.*)

The joys of heaven and the pains of hell in the future life are depicted in vivid manner, and warnings are given to unbelievers of a dire future:

HEAVEN
> All who believe in Allah and His Prophet shall be admitted hereafter into the delightful gardens (Paradise). They shall repose forever on couches decked with gold and precious stones, being supplied with abundance of luscious wine, fruits of the choicest variety, and the flesh of birds. They shall be accompanied by damsels of unsurpassed beauty, with large black, pearl-like eyes. (*Meccan Suras, 56.*)

HELL
> We will make the path to happiness easy and safe to all such as fear Allah, and give alms, and believe the truth proclaimed by Allah's messenger. But we will make easy the path to distress and misery for all such as are niggardly, are bent on making riches, and deny the truth when it is proclaimed to them. When these last fall headlong into Hell, their wealth will avail them nothing. In the burning furnace they shall burn and broil. (*Meccan Suras, 92.*)

Although the Koran is planless and fragmentary, there emerges a set of principles and practices that forms the basis of the religion. The principles may be summarized as follows:

One God: The unity of God is emphasized. The Christian doctrine of the Trinity is rejected. "Do not say there are three Gods — Allah, Isa (Jesus), and Mary. There is but one God, and He can have no son." Allah, it is written, is surrounded by angels — pure, sexless beings who bear the throne and praise him continually. He is the apotheosis of power, unity, and goodness.

Creation: The Koran accepts the Hebrew concept of the creation of the world in six days, as well as the story of the temptation of Adam in Paradise. Between men and angels are Jinn, male and female devils created from fire.

Prophets: The revelation of God to man has come through three great prophets: Moses, who gave the Law; Jesus, who gave the Gospel; and Muhammad, the last and greatest of the three, who gave the Koran. The mission of Muhammad was to warn all men of the coming judgment.

Taboos: Muslims, like the Hebrews, are not allowed to eat pork. Moreover, all Muslims are forbidden to touch intoxicating liquors. They are permitted no altars, images, or pictures of any kind in the houses of prayer. The mosques in Damascus, Jerusalem, Cairo, and Constantinople are richly colored with marbles, mosaics, stained-glass windows, and intricate rugs, but they contain no images.

The five practices of Islam are:

Creed: Every Muslim must participate in reciting the creed aloud: "There is no God but Allah and Muhammad is his chief apostle!" He must indicate a "full understanding" of its meaning and must in his heart recognize its truth.

Prayer: God must be worshiped five times each day — at dawn or just before sunrise, immediately after noon, before sunset, after sunset, and after the day has closed. Detailed physical positions are prescribed for each part of the service. Prayer must be preceded by washing of face, hands (to the elbows), and feet, and the believer must always face *qibla*, the direction of prayer toward Mecca.

Fasting: During the month of Ramadan (when, according to the lunar calendar, the Koran was revealed), every Muslim must endure a severe fast lasting from sunrise to sunset each day of the sacred month. If one is on a journey or if he is ill, he can abstain from food and drink "another number of days." If he fails to fast, he can redeem himself by feeding a poor man; "but if ye fast, it is better for you."

Almsgiving: The Koran recommends almsgiving as a major tenet of Islamic practice. Legal alms are to be given in cattle, grain, or money once a year after a year's possession; exact percentages are prescribed, such as a tenth of grain or fruit if watered by rain and a twentieth if the result of irrigation. Voluntary alms are left to the conscience of believers.

Pilgrimage to Mecca: A pilgrimage to Mecca should be made at least once in his lifetime by each Muslim. When arriving within five or six miles of the holy city, everyone, whether rich or poor, dons the same type of ceremonial dress. He abstains from shaving or trimming the nails; proceeds to the sacred mosque, where he kisses the black stone in the *Kaaba*; and then encircles the holy relic seven times, three times running and four times slowly walking.

Muhammad and the religion of Islam strongly influenced the course of world civilization. As a result of Muslim conquests, the Byzantine Empire lost most of its possessions in Asia and Africa and was reduced to a small, comparatively weak state. The spread of Islam brought the whole Western world, stretching from Spain through the Orient, into close commercial relations. Although it was destined to disintegrate speedily, the Muslim Empire brought an enormous intellectual stimulation to the entire world west of China.

Islam converted many millions, who, if it had not existed, might have turned to Christianity. Indirectly, however, the march of Islam had some beneficial effects upon Roman Catholic Christianity. Eastern Christianity suffered most intensely from Islamic rivalry, leaving the Roman pope as undisputed head of the Church in the West and lessening the spiritual powers of the patriarch at Constantinople. The power of Islam and of the papacy grew in strength simultaneously and independently, and did not come into open conflict until the Crusades.

The Muslim spirit, flashing across the Western world in brilliant if brief fashion, formed a bond of union between ancient and modern civilizations. The Muslim mind kept the spirit of scientific learning alive and maintained it, until by the Renaissance the spark of genius appeared elsewhere. The effect of Muslim influence on Western civilization may be measured in part by the many words of Arabic origin now part of the English language.

Once again we see a major turning point in history stimulated by the emergence of a prophet who called on men to worship one God and to flee from the wrath to come. These ideas were not entirely strange: there were many Christians and Jews in Arabia, and Muhammad borrowed liberally from their beliefs. It was said that Muhammad used three weapons — a tongue, a whip, and a sword, but that he only used the second or third when the first failed. To millions of his followers he was a God-inspired prophet who showed them the way to paradise. Muslims today regard him as the ideal human being on earth, the supreme example of a man of all seasons.

BATTLE OF TOURS, 732 A.D.

*"Then all the host fled before the enemy,
and many died in the flight."*

A CLASH between the two great religions — expanding Christendom and spreading Islam — was not long in coming. Advocates of the predictability thesis will say "I told you so!" but there was no absolute necessity for the confrontation. Yet, it took place and it became a major turning point in history.

The battle of Tours in 732 A.D. was the first important setback suffered by the Muslims in their movement westward. Had they been successful, the history of Western Europe as well as that of the entire world would have taken on a different coloration. Instead, the tide of Muslim conquest receded into Spain. Western Europe retained Catholic Christianity in the medieval milieu.

We have seen how the faith of Muhammad originated in humble fashion and how it gathered momentum, supplanting Christianity in many lands. The Arabs of Western Asia swept westward across northern Africa and into Spain while their brothers surged eastward into India and China. The advance in both directions was so rapid that within the course of a century, a huge Muslim empire spread from the borders of India to the Atlantic, and from the Caspian Sea to the Indian Ocean. Islam became a powerful rival of Christianity in the west.

Before his death Muhammad counseled his followers to go forth and preach the faith of Islam: "Those who shall refuse shall be humbled." He commanded a sacred war (*jihad*) against unbelievers: "I swear by God in whose hand is my life, that marching about morning and evening to fight for religion is better than the world and everything in it. And verily the presence of one of you in line of battle is better than all sorts of extra prayers in your own house for sixty years."

During his lifetime Muhammad had supreme political and spiritual control over his followers, but after his death a struggle took place for the succession, finally culminating in the election of his friend and helper, Abu Bakr, as caliph (successor). The immediate successors to Muhammad were able to maintain a semblance of unity in their vast realm, despite separatist movements, and within twenty years after the death of the Prophet they brought Syria, Egypt, Babylonia, and Persia under the rule of Islam.

The success of Muslim expansion cannot be explained merely by religious motivation. The transformation of Islam from a purely tribal faith into one of the great universal religions may be attributed to a number of factors. Discontented with unfavorable environment, the tribes of Arabia looked toward the fertile lands in the north and the rich lands of Egypt as areas of exploitation. Like the Germanic barbarians before them, they were attracted by a better climate and by prospects of wealth. Various political factors were allied to this economic motive. The caliphs, realizing that the maintenance of unity in the Arabian peninsula was a different matter, offered to their followers promises of plunder beyond their wildest dreams. Moveover, they were certain that the Byzantine and Persian Empires, engaged in costly wars, were ripe for conquest. The morale of the two empires to the north had been almost destroyed – the people were on the verge of revolt because of unpopular taxation and were not inclined to fight in defense of their regimes.

The religious motive was a convenient pretext. Assured by the words of the Prophet that death on the battlefield against unbelievers would bring them to an eternal life of pleasure in the gardens of Paradise, the Arabs fought with reckless courage. Westerners were almost helpless when faced with these warriors. Yet, the Muslims did not always seek to convert the conquered by the sword, despite the popular belief to the contrary. The vanquished peoples might either accept the Koran, or maintain their own religion and pay tribute in lieu of military service, or refuse both terms and be put to the sword as rebels and traitors. Actually, the Arabs were regarded often as liberators by those subjugated peoples who found it advantageous to embrace the faith. Muslim promises of religious freedom and liberal treatment led the people of one city after another to surrender to the invaders and even to welcome them.

After making themselves masters of the Arabian peninsula, the Arabs set out to conquer the Byzantine and Persian Empires, which had been fighting among themselves and in 628 had concluded a peace of exhaustion. The Byzantine emperor, Heraclius, had just reconquered Syria and Egypt, but weakened by dropsy and faced by religious revolts in the conquered territories, he was in no condition to withstand the tide of Muslim conquest. The masses in Syria were Semitic-speaking and hence more friendly to the Arabs than to the Greeks at Constantinople; moreover, the Syrians objected to Byzantine taxation. The Arabs captured Damascus, chief city of Syria, and took Jerusalem and Caesarea. They were even more successful in Egypt. Here, as in the north, the tax-burdened people and heretical Christian sects welcomed the Arabs enthusiastically. Large elements were converted to Islam.

Meanwhile, the Arab invaders, who had taken to the sea, captured Cyprus and Rhodes. Then they began a series of attacks upon Constantinople by sea and by land. Constantinople, well fortified and strongly defended, held out against the invaders. Repeated sea attacks were unsuccessful.

The Arabs turned eastward during this period and then added the whole of the Tigris-Euphrates Valley to the rapidly growing Muslim state. They pushed into western Turkestan and still farther until they met the Chinese. As long as they paid regular tribute, the conquered Byzantine and Persian peoples (including Christians and Jews) were permitted to retain their own institutions. Certain to have the amount of their tribute reduced drastically if they embraced the faith of Muhammad, millions accepted the new religion.

With the faith that moves mountains, Muslim conquerors decided to seek the domination of the whole Western European world. Their conquest of North Africa was less rapid than that of the Byzantine and Persian Empires. It took half a century before North Africa fell to Muslim domination. Here the Berber tribes, whose zeal for fighting equaled that of the Arab invaders, resisted and delayed the conquest, but they were finally overthrown, accepted Islam, and joined the westward tide of conquest. The city of Carthage fell by 700. The invaders poured westward through Algeria and Morocco to the Atlantic.

After the conversion of the Berbers and Moors, the combined warriors decided to drive on northward into Europe by way of Spain. In 711 Muslim General Tariq crossed the strait and landed in Spain near the famous promontory that has been named for him (Gibraltar — Gabal-Tariq — Mount of Tariq). The Muslims overcame the Visigothic forces, and within several years all Spain, with the exception of the northern coastline, was under the control of the Muslim ruler at Toledo. The conquest of Spain was facilitated by internal dissensions in the Visigothic kingdom. The oppressed peasantry and the persecuted Jews welcomed the Muslim conquerors, whose reputation for tolerance and generosity had preceded them.

The Muslim invaders used the region south of the Pyrenees as a base for operations against Gaul. While their eastern co-religionists hammered at the gates of Constantinople, the western Arabs were preparing for the conquest of Western Europe. But here the expanding Muslim power was to come into conflict with the Franks, who were also consolidating and expanding a large kingdom. Arabs and Franks — Muslims and Christians — headed straight for confrontation.

Who were the Franks and how did they form an obstacle to the fast-moving Arabs? The Frankish kingdom reached its greatest height in the century from the reign of Charles Martel, beginning in 714, to the death of the greatest Frank, Charlemagne, in 814. In 687 Pepin II, who was a powerful Austrasian noble, united Neustria and Austrasia, thus checking the tendency toward division in Francia, and made the office of Mayor of the Palace hereditary. Although not designated by his father as successor, Charles, an illegitimate son of Pepin II, proceeded to unify the Frankish dominions. A man of relentless energy and military genius, he was determined to make his power felt throughout the whole territory by reducing to obedience the many bishops, dukes, and counts who were attempting to make themselves supreme in their own districts. One by one the rebellious overlords of Burgundy, Aquitaine, Bavaria, and Alemannia were compelled to acknowledge the overlordship of Charles. When the Muslims crossed the Pyrenees into Gaul, they found Charles overlord of Europe north of the Alps from the Pyrenees to Hungary and ruling over a multitude of lords speaking French-Latin and High and Low German. They were to learn the hard way that this was no minor enemy astride their path of conquest.

In the summer of 732 the Muslims advanced into Gaul. They were commanded by Abderrahman, described by Arab writers as a model of integrity. During the two years of his second administration in Spain, he reformed many governmental abuses, and made preparations for a campaign to conquer Gaul. Arab chroniclers rate his army at only 80,000 men, but Christian writers swell its numbers to hundreds of thousands more. Little is known about his army except that most of it was composed of Muslims and many were mounted. They seldom wore armor, preferring instead the lance and sword. The combat troops were followed by mules loaded with plunder, as well as by a nondescript rabble. The army lived by ransacking the countryside. In battle it moved ahead in fierce, undisciplined charges.

The invading Muslims won a quick victory near Bordeaux over Eudo, Duke of Aquitaine. They then pushed forward toward Orléans, plundering as they went. At Poitiers they destroyed the basilica of St. Hilary. Loaded with loot, they turned to Tours, where they were attracted by the enormous wealth of the church of St. Martin.

At Tours the invading host was faced not with Eudo and his weak army, but with the powerful Frankish ruler, Charles. The Frankish army, relying mostly upon infantry, was composed of two groups: the General's private army, which received only plunder for its services, and a local badly armed militia. The private army had been blooded many times in combat, but the militia had little understanding of the arts of discipline or battle.

Charles, an able general, understood his Muslim enemy. According to Gibbon, he had already written to Eudo:

> If you follow my advice you will not interrupt their march nor precipitate your attack. They are like a torrent, which it is dangerous to stem in its career. The thirst of riches and the consciousness of success, redouble their valor, and valor is of more avail than arms or numbers. Be patient till they have loaded themselves with the encumbrances of wealth. The possession of wealth will divide their counsels and assure your victory.

Apparently, this shrewd advice did not help Eudo. Monkish chroniclers attest to the terror inspired by the Muslim invasion. Rumors flew throughout Gaul that the Muslims were pouring in from Spain with their wives and children, in such multitudes that no man could reckon or estimate them. "They brought with them all their armor, and whatever they had, as if they were thenceforth always to dwell in France."

The sudden appearance of Charles and his army caused consternation among the Muslims, by this time loaded down with loot and almost immobile. Abderrahman played with the idea of abandoning the plunder, but he knew that his men would refuse to obey him if he gave such an order.

It was October 732, just a hundred years after the death of Muhammad. For seven days the two armies sat facing one another. Abderrahman sent a part of his plunder southward, while Charles waited the arrival of more troops.

There are few details of the battle itself. It is not even certain as to where it was fought — the armies came into contact somewhere near Tours. The Muslims fell back toward Poitiers, where Abderrahman decided to accept battle in order to cover his withdrawal. Charles drew up his army in a solid phalanx.

As usual with the Muslims, combat opened with a cavalry charge. The light Arab horsemen dashed toward the Frankish army, which, in the words of Isidorus Pacensis, was an "immovable wall," firm as "a rock of ice." The cavalry attacked again and again, only to be pushed back by the stolid Frankish phalanx.

Toward the end of the evening, Eudo and his Aquitanians managed to turn one of the Muslim flanks. An attack was then launched on Abderrahman's camp, in which the bulk of the remaining Arab loot was cached. The Muslims, abandoning their booty, began to fall back. Abderrahman himself was killed in the close-quarter fighting.

The next morning Charles drew up his army to meet another attack. His scouts reported that the Muslim camp had been abandoned. Panicked by the loss of their leader, the Muslims fled south and left nearly all their plunder behind them.

Charles did not pursue the fleeing enemy because his own men were laden down with booty and scarcely had the mobility for further marches. Moreover, the mounted Muslims were far too fast for his infantry. In addition, as a matter of political expediency, he did not want to relieve Eudo completely from Muslim pressure.

A surprisingly objective account of the battle came from one of the Arab chroniclers, who was quite willing to grant the Frankish victory:

> Near the river Owar (Loire), the two great hosts of the two languages and the two creeds were set in array against each other. The hearts of Abderrahman, his captains, and his men were filled with wrath and pride, and they were first to begin to fight. The Muslim horsemen dashed fiercely and frequently forward against the battalions of the Franks, who resisted manfully, and many fell dead on either side, until the going down of the sun. Night parted the two armies.
>
> In the gray of the morning the Muslims returned to the battle. Their cavaliers had soon hewn their way into the center of the Christian host. But many of the Muslims were fearful for the safety of the spoil which they had stored in their tents, and a false cry arose in their ranks that some of the enemy were plundering

the camp. Whereupon several squadrons of the Muslim horsemen rode off to protect their tents. But it seemed as if they fled; and all the host was troubled. And while Abderrahman strove to check their tumult, and to lead them back to battle, the warriors of the Franks came around him, and he was pierced through with many spears, and so that he died.

Then all the host fled before the enemy, and many died in the flight. This deadly defeat of the Muslims, and the loss of the great leader and good cavalier, Abderrahman, took place in the hundred and fifteenth year [of the *Hegira*]. [1]

Monkish chroniclers, overcome by the meaning of the conflict, gave fantastic casualties. One stated that the Arabs lost 375,000 men, while only 1007 Christians fell, which he explained was due to the special interposition of Providence. The casualties could not possibly have been so high: there was not enough food for such a mighty host, certainly not to stay around for seven days before committing itself to battle.

So ended the great Muslim invasion of Western Europe. Retiring to Spain, the Muslims settled down to consolidate their already huge empire. Although they again tried to move beyond the Pyrenees, they were never successful in extending their influence into Gaul.

Charles, his son, and his grandson were left to consolidate the Frankish empire. Christendom, though still disunited, was safe. For his crushing victory Charles was given the title of Martel ("Hammer") — the savior of Christendom against the Muslims.

Gibbon gave a pessimistic picture of what might have happened had not the Muslims been stopped at Tours:

A victorious line of march had been prolonged above a thousand miles from the rock of Gibraltar to the banks of the Loire; the repetition of an equal space would have carried the Saracens to the confines of Poland and the Highlands of Scotland. The Rhine is not more impassable than the Nile or Euphrates, and the Arabian fleet might have sailed without a naval combat into the mouth of the Thames. Perhaps the interpretation of the Koran would now be taught in the schools of Oxford, and her pupils might demonstrate to a circumcised people the sanctity and truth of the revelation of Muhammad.

---

[1] The Arab was five years off in his reckoning. The *Hegira* took place in 622 A.D., one hundred and ten years earlier.

CORONATION OF CHARLEMAGNE, 800 A.D.

"This demand King Charles would not refuse."

TURNING points do not necessarily lead upward to a higher plane, for history is concerned with the development of man rather than his progress. At times the mainstream may turn and head back in the direction from which it came. Among such events was the coronation of Charlemagne in 800 A.D., described by James Bryce as "the central event of the Middle Ages." Here was a deliberate attempt to turn back to the glorious days of the Roman Empire, to re-create that empire and its *Pax Romana* which held Western civilization in a viselike grip of order and security. At the same time the coronation marked the beginning of a long struggle between the temporal and spiritual heads of the Western world.

Charlemagne (r. 768-814 A.D.), whose name is the French form for the Latin *Carolus Magnus* (Charles the Great), was the first Frankish leader of whom we have any satisfactory knowledge. Einhard (or Eginhard), companion and secretary, described his master in his *Vita Caroli Magni.* Probably inaccurate in spots, it did give an absorbing portrait of the great man. Several passages are condensed here:

> In accordance with the national custom, he took frequent exercise on horseback and in the chase, in which sports scarcely any people in the world can equal the Franks. He was temperate in eating, and especially so in drinking. While at the table, he listened to reading or music, the subjects of the readings being the stories and deeds of olden time. He had the gift of ready and fluent speech, and could express whatever he had to say with the utmost clearness, so eloquent indeed was he that he might have been taken for a teacher of oratory.
>
> He most zealously cherished the liberal arts, held those that taught them in great esteem, and conferred great honors on them. He spent much time and

labor studying rhetoric, dialectic, and especially astronomy. He also tried to write, and used to keep tablets and blanks in bed under his pillow, that at leisure hours he might accustom his hand to form the letters; however, as he began his efforts late in life, and not at the proper time, he met with little success.

He cherished with the greatest fervor and devotion the principles of the Christian religion, which had been instilled in him from infancy. He took great pains to improve the church reading and singing, for he was well skilled in both, although he neither read in public nor sang, except in a low tone with others. He cared for the Church of St. Peter the Apostle at Rome above all other holy and sacred places, and heaped high its treasury with a vast wealth of gold, silver, and precious stones.

As conqueror, administrator, and patron of culture Charlemagne left his mark on Western civilization. A crop of legends has grown around his name. In the *chansons de geste,* medieval songs of valor, Charlemagne was depicted in romantic, if unhistorical, fashion as the heroic leader who gave the age of chivalry its quality. Certainly he understood the milieu of his time and met his problems with consummate energy. Charlemagne ranks with the great political leaders of history.

When he ascended the throne, Charlemagne had undisputed claim to the Frankish dominions. But he began a campaign that was to bring him into conflict with almost every important people in Europe. His intention was to bring all the Germanic peoples together into one great Christian empire and to protect it against the Slavs on the east and the Muslims to the south. These were formidable tasks even for a Charlemagne.

For thirty-three years Charlemagne carried on warfare against the heathen Saxons, who stubbornly resisted all efforts to Christianize them. Clinging to their ancient institutions, the proud Saxons retired behind strong national defenses (the hills and forests of Teutoburger Wald and the wild Harz country) and played a waiting game. Charlemagne came after them summer after summer (the Saxons were available for battle only during warm weather), and converted as many as possible. The Saxon technique was to offer submission when Charlemagne was in their district, massacre the churchmen he left behind, and then destroy Christian property. The Frankish leader met this custom with a savage technique of his own: on one occasion as an object lesson he put to the sword 4,500 unarmed Saxon captives in one day. After establishing strongholds in Saxon territory, he divided the lands into bishoprics and then decreed special laws providing for fierce penalties against violations, such as death for a Saxon if he entered a church by violence, or execution if he ate meat during Lent.

Charlemagne entered into an alliance with the papacy to protect Italy from the Lombards. He experimented with the weapon of marriage, taking the daughter of Desiderius, King of the Lombards, as wife in 770. The next year he repudiated the Lombard princess and married Hildegarde, a Swabian lady. Desiderius, resenting the jilting of his daughter and observing that Charlemagne was busy in Saxony, attacked the papacy in central Italy. Upon Pope Hadrian's appeal for help, Charlemagne crossed the Alps with a great army, subdued Desiderius, and then took the title "King of the Lombards" for himself. Continuing on to Rome, he was acclaimed "Patrician of the Romans." The Frankish king was demonstrating his deep love for his faith.

Charlemagne now turned on the hordes of Slavs and Avars who were menacing his eastern borders. He harried their settlements, repelled their armies, sacked their camps, forced them to pay tribute, and converted many of them to Christianity.

Perceiving disaffection among the Muslims who had settled in northern Spain, Charlemagne decided to lead an expedition against them. He was not at first successful, losing his famous aide, Count Roland of Brittany, who fell at Ronces-vaux (or Roncesvalles) with other warriors on August 15, 778. This event passed into legend and song in the celebrated *Song of Roland,* the great epic poem of early French literature. Charlemagne's conquest of the Muslims came many centuries before their expulsion from Spain, which culminated in the fall of Granada in 1492.

A rival faction accused Pope Leo III of both perjury and adultery, and tried to drive him from the papal throne. Assaulted on the streets of Rome, he managed to escape his attackers, but he was imprisoned for a time in a Roman monastery. Making his way northward across the Alps, Leo appeared at the court of Charle-magne, who, though busy with his rebellious Saxons, pledged his help. Charlemagne appeared at Rome in November, 800.

While kneeling at the alter of St. Peter's on Christmas Day, 800 A.D., Charle-magne was approached by the Pope, crowned, and saluted as "Emperor of the Romans." Although annoyed by the circumstances of his coronation, about which he probably had no previous knowledge and which signified the overlordship of the papacy, Charlemagne, nevertheless, gracefully accepted the honor. An old Frankish account in the *Annals of Lauresheim* explains the reasons for Leo's act:

> And as the title of Emperor had then come to an end among the Greeks, who were under the rule of a woman, it seemed to Pope Leo himself and to all the holy fathers present at the council, as well as to the rest of the Christian people, that they ought to give the rank of emperor to Charles, King of the Franks, who held Rome itself, where the Caesars had ever been wont to dwell, as well as other places in Italy, Gaul, and Germany. Since almighty God had put all these places in his power, it seemed to them but right that, in accordance with the demand of the Christian people, he should have the title also. This demand King Charles would not refuse; but, submitting in all humility to God, at the prayer of the clergy and of the whole Christian people, he received the title of Emperor together with consecration from Pope Leo.

For Charlemagne it was a kind of promotion. He had come to Rome merely as *Rex Francorum* (King of the Franks), controlling only Gaul, Germany, and Lombardy. He left the imperial city as *Imperator Romanorum* (Emperor of the Romans), with sovereignty over the whole West, including Africa, Spain, and England. But actually, the Frankish kingdom still remained the core of his empire.

After the coronation Charlemagne retired to Aachen (Aix-la-Chapelle) in his homeland, where the forests gave him good hunting and where he could bathe and swim in the hot springs. He maintained his interest in theology and always considered himself a good son of the Church. If the Pope had any objection to Charlemagne's private life, he never gave it public notice. Although Charlemagne was a devoted husband to three of his four wives, he had illegitimate offspring by five mistresses.

The revived empire was supposed to be a continuation of the Roman Empire of Augustus. Later, in the twelfth century, it was titled the Holy Roman Empire by Frederick Barbarossa, the Hohenstaufen. It was to endure in theory until 1806 when Napoleon claimed the right of succession for himself. In practice, the Holy Roman Empire from 1556 (abdication of Charles V) to 1806 was only a loose confederation of lay and ecclesiastical German princes. For the German rulers the coronation meant a long, futile struggle for supremacy over Italy. Many Germans were to lose their lives in vain efforts to obtain the shadowy crown at Rome for one pretender or another.

The Carolingian Empire did not long survive its founder. Held together for a short time by Charlemagne's son Louis the Pious, it was divided by the Treaty of Verdun in 843 A.D. into three parts — Charles the Bald got what is roughly today France; Louis the German obtained Germany; and Lothair the Italian received the Italian peninsula, and the so-called *Zwischenland* — Alsace and Lorraine. Thus began the outlines of three modern European states. For more than 1100 years French and Germans fought over that "in-between land" of Alsace-Lorraine; yet the unobservant Italians have never laid claim to an area which seems historically to have been awarded to them.

After the futile Carolingian attempt to turn back the clock, Western Europe sank into the lethargy of feudalism.

CRUSADES: THE SPEECH OF URBAN II, 1095

"It is the will of God! It is the will of God"

HISTORIANS, a notoriously thin-skinned lot, often deny the right of a first-rate journalist to enter their ranks. They are inclined to overlook the fact that among others the able journalist Allan Nevins became a most distinguished American historian. They enjoy taking pot shots at Toynbee, who takes equal pleasure in making sarcastic responses to their challenges..

Even more vociferous is the reaction of virtually all professional historians to Carlyle's great-man theory of history — that historical development hinges upon the personality and actions of outstanding leaders. The time, they say, is all-important, the man is insignificant; if Napoleon had not lived there would have been another to take his place. Certainly it is easy to overemphasize the role of the activist in promoting historical change, yet on occasion the action of a single man may well give direction to a turning point in history.

A case is that of the Crusades, that series of campaigns or religious wars undertaken by the Christians of Western Europe from 1096 to 1291 in the name of the Church for the purpose of recovering the Holy Land from the Muslims. This was a major turning point not only in the history of the Church but also in the whole course of Western civilization.

The Crusades may be regarded from two viewpoints: first, as an extension of the period of religious revival that had surged through Western Europe in the tenth and eleventh centuries; and, second, as a key development in the relations between West and East. In the first sense, the Crusades reflected the power of the Cluniac revival, which encouraged pilgrimages to Jerusalem, as well as the desire of the papacy to purify the Church and to direct the feudal interest in warfare to the Holy Land. In the second sense, the Crusades revived the ancient religous feud between West and East on an incomparably greater scale. The threat of Muslim expansion in Europe was continually present; against it the Crusades appeared as a protection of Europe against the renascence of Muslim power by the Seljuk Turks.

The Crusades as "holy wars" were symptomatic of the new energy of life in Western society, just emerging out of feudal disorder. They were a failure in one important military respect: they ended not in the conquest of the East by the West, but in the loss of the Byzantine Empire and nearly all of southeastern Europe to the Turkish Muslims. Despite this, they exerted a strong influence upon history from nearly every point of view. They undoubtedly hastened the coming of modern civilization.

The movement was touched off in November 1095, when Pope Urban II called a council of churchmen and feudal nobles at Clermont. After discussing matters of ecclesiastical policy, he delivered a remarkable address designed to arouse the fighting instincts of his audience. It was one of the most dramatic speeches of history: [1]

Oh, race of Franks, race beyond the mountains [the Alps], race beloved and chosen by God (as is clear from many of your works), set apart from all other nations by the situation of your country, as well as by your Catholic faith and the honor you render to the holy Church: to you our discourse is addressed, and for you our exhortations are intended. We wish you to know what a serious matter has led us to your country, for it is the imminent peril threatening you and all the faithful that has brought us hither.

From the confines of Jerusalem and from the city of Constantinople a grievous report has gone forth and has been brought repeatedly to our ears; namely, that a race from the kingdom of the Persians, an accursed race, a race wholly alienated from God, "a generation that set not their heart aright, and whose spirit was not steadfast with God" [Ps., lxxviii. 8], has violently invaded the lands of those Christians and has depopulated them by pillage and fire. They have led away a part of the captives into their own country, and a part they have killed by cruel tortures. They have either destroyed the churches of God or appropriated them for the rites of their own religion. They destroy the altars, after having defiled them with their uncleanness. . . . The kingdom of the Greeks [the Eastern Empire] is now dismembered by them and has been deprived of territory so vast in extent that it could not be traversed in two months' time.

On whom, therefore, rests the labor of avenging these wrongs and of recovering this territory, if not upon you — you, upon whom, above all other nations, God has conferred remarkable glory in arms, great courage, bodily activity, and strength to humble the heads of those who resist you? Let the deeds of your ancestors encourage you and incite your minds to manly achievements — the glory and greatness of King Charlemagne, and of his son Louis [the Pious], and

---

[1] Adapted from translation by Dana C. Munro, in *University of Pennsylvania Translations and Reprints*, Vol. 1, No. 2, pp. 5-8.

of your other monarchs, who have destroyed the kingdom of the Turks and have extended the sway of the holy Church over lands previously pagan. Let the holy sepulcher of our Lord and Saviour, which is possessed by the unclean nations, especially arouse you, and the holy places which are now treated with ignominy and irreverently polluted with the filth of the unclean. Oh most valiant soldiers and descendants of invincible ancestors, do not degenerate, but recall the valor of your ancestors.

But if you are hindered by love of children, parents, or wife, remember what the Lord says in the Gospel, "He that loveth father or mother more than me is not worthy of me" [Matt., x.37]. "Every one that hath forsaken houses, or brethren, or sisters, or father, or mother, or wife, or children, or lands, for my name's sake, shall receive an hundred-fold, and shall inherit everlasting life" [Matt., xix.29]. Let none of your possessions restrain you, nor anxiety for your family affairs. For this land which you inhabit, shut in on all sides by the seas and surrounded by the mountain peaks, is too narrow for your large population; nor does it abound in wealth; and it furnishes scarcely food enough for its cultivators. Hence it is that you murder and devour one another, that you wage war, and that very many among you perish in civil strife.

Let hatred, therefore, depart from among you; let your quarrels end; let wars cease; and let all dissensions and controversies slumber. Enter upon the road of the Holy Sepulcher; wrest that land from the wicked race, and subject it to yourselves. That land which, as the Scripture says, "floweth with milk and honey" [Num., xiii. 27] was given by God into the power of the children of Israel. Jerusalem is the center of the earth; the land is fruitful above all others, like another paradise of delights. This spot the Redeemer of mankind has made illustrious by His advent, has beautified by His sojourn, has consecrated by His passion, has redeemed by His death, has glorified by His burial.

This royal city, however, situated at the center of the earth, is now held captive by the enemies of Christ and is subjected, by those who do not know God, to the worship of the heathen. She seeks, therefore, and desires to be liberated, and ceases not to implore you to come to her aid. From you especially she asks succor, because, as we have already said, God has conferred upon you, above all other nations, great glory in arms. Accordingly, undertake this journey eagerly for the remission of your sins, with the assurance of the reward of imperishable glory in the kingdom of heaven.

[When Pope Urban had skilfully said these and very many similar things, he so centered in one purpose the desires of all who were present that all cried out, "It is the will of God! It is the will of God!" When the venerable Roman pontiff heard that, with eyes uplifted to heaven, he gave thanks to God and, commanding silence with his hand, said:]

Most beloved brethren, to-day is manifest in you what the Lord says in the Gospel, "Where two or three are gathered together in my name, there am I in the midst of them" [Matt., xviii. 20]. For unless God had been present in your spirits, all of you would not have uttered the same cry; since, although the cry issued from numerous mouths, yet the origin of the cry was one. Therefore I say to you that God, who implanted this in your breasts, has drawn it forth from you. Let that, then, be your war cry in battle, because it is given to you by God.

When an armed attack is made upon the enemy, let this one cry be raised by all the soldiers of God: "It is the will of God! It is the will of God!"

And we neither command nor advise that the old or feeble, or those incapable of bearing arms, undertake this journey. Nor ought women to set out at all without their husbands, or brothers, or legal guardians. For such are more of a hindrance than aid, more of a burden than an advantage. Let the rich aid the needy; and according to their wealth let them take with them experienced soldiers. The priests and other clerks [clergy], whether secular or regular, are not to go without the consent of their bishop; for this journey would profit them nothing if they went without permission. Also, it is not fitting that laymen should enter upon the pilgrimage without the blessing of their priests.

Whoever, therefore, shall decide upon this holy pilgrimage, and shall make his vow to God to that effect, and shall offer himself to Him for sacrifice, as a living victim, holy and acceptable to God, shall wear the sign of the cross of the Lord on his forehead or on his breast. When he shall return from his journey, having fulfilled his vow, let him place the cross on his back between his shoulders. Thus shall ye, indeed, by this twofold action, fulfill the precept of the Lord, as He commands in the Gospel, "He that taketh not his cross, and followeth after me, is not worthy of me" [*Luke*, xiv. 27].

Pope Urban's extraordinary appeal started the long series of enterprises to the East, from the People's Crusade of 1096 to the Eighth Crusade of 1270–1272. Thousands, filled with fanatical enthusiasm, set forth to the Holy Land with scarcely any thought of how they were to get there. The movement took on the tenor of revivalist meetings. People anxious to find respite from their troubles set off toward the East as if to a newly discovered El Dorado. "It was," wrote Ernest Barker, "a stream carrying in its turbid waters much refuse, tramps, and bankrupts, camp-followers and hucksters, fugitive monks and escaped villeins, and marked by the same motley grouping, the same fever of life, the same alternations of affluence and beggary, which marked the rush for a gold-field today."

In 1212 came what has been called one of the most ghastly tragedies in history – the Children's Crusade. A French shepherd boy named Stephen proclaimed that he was commanded by God to lead an army of children to rescue the Holy Sepulcher. He vowed that he would lead his boyish army from a wagon southward to Marseilles, where the sea would open so that he could bring his followers dry-shod across the Mediterranean. Simultaneously, in Germany a youngster from Cologne named Nicholas gathered youthful followers in like fashion and led them into Italy. Some 50,000 childish innocents were persuaded in a hypnotic trance to follow their Pied Pipers of Hamelin straight into the jaws of death.

It was a catastrophe. Stephen's army was kidnapped by slave merchants and sold in Egypt. Most of Nicholas's expedition went to their death. Pope Innocent III misjudged the expeditions: "The very children put us to shame. While we sleep they go forth gladly to conquer the Holy Land."

One crusade followed another after this melancholy affair. On May 18, 1291, the last Christian post in the Holy Land was stormed by the Sultan Kelaun, and its defenders captured, massacred, or sold into slavery. So ended the Crusades, nearly two centuries from the time when they began.

The Crusades affected every field of Western society. From the economic point of view they led to the growth of commerce. During the early Middle Ages, the volume of trade between East and West had fallen well below that existing during the late Roman Empire. Frequent contact of the West with the East during the Crusades stimulated the demand for such Oriental goods as sugar, spices, silks, cottons, muslins, satins, jewelry, and perfumes. The crusader who brought Oriental products with him on his return unconsciously propagandized the wealth and luxury of the East. There were fortunes to be made in meeting the European demand for Oriental goods.

In order to purchase products from the Levant, it became increasingly necessary to obtain money. Those who continued to trade by payment in kind could not get products from Eastern merchants, for the latter demanded metallic currency. Banks were organized thoughout Europe and a credit system was constructed, leading eventually to the building of a money economy. It was inconvenient to transport large sums over routes infested with pirates and brigands. Instead, checks, bills of exchange, and money drafts were used. Moreover, the crusaders needed financial credits before starting out on an expedition to the Holy Land. The banking houses of northern Italy accumulated great wealth by lending money to crusaders and merchants.

Such Italian cities as Venice, Genoa, Pisa, Amalfi, and Palermo enjoyed a boom period during the Crusades. Crusaders usually stopped at these ports to obtain funds, supplies, and means of transportation. Trade with the East led to enormous profits. The Italian cities became rich and laid a firm basis for their cultural dominance in the Renaissance. Commodities poured in from the East, to be diffused across the Brenner Pass and down the Rhine to Bruges. Along this route the great towns of the Middle Ages sprang up as if by magic.

As the towns increased in size and as the merchants became more prosperous, it became necessary to improve methods of navigation and to build bigger and better ships. The compass was improved, sea charts made, and travel books — "medieval Baedekers" — were used to guide the crusaders and pilgrims on their journeys. Regular sea lanes were provided for Christian tourists and merchants. Huge galleys were constructed to carry many hundreds of passengers and to bring back Oriental wares at comparatively small freight rates. The drive eastward led eventually to the discovery of the interior of Asia.

Many crusaders turned to Jews to obtain necessary funds for their expeditions. Partly because of their position as moneylenders and partly because of fanatical Christian crusading zeal, the Jews were subjected to persecution. With the growth of a Christian mercantile class, the Jews were excluded from commerce and eventually from all other professions in the greater part of Europe. Forced to employ their capital in the only way left open to them — that is, by lending at interest — they aroused intense hostility. The whole of the Crusades was a long martyrdom for the Jews.

Added to these economic factors were important political results. Although the Crusades were not alone responsible for the decline of feudalism, they contributed in part to its disintegration. The departure of many powerful lords to the East tended to weaken the most influential element in feudal society. Hundreds of male heirs to baronial estates were killed in the Holy Land; the result was increased power for the centralized authority in the feudal arrangement.

There were also profound religious changes. The influence of the papacy grew enormously at first as a result of the early Crusades. At the accession of Urban II, the reform policy of the Church had made little headway, and consequently, the entire organization of Christendom was in a precarious state. Urban seized the opportunity for leadership of the First Crusade. From then on, with several exceptions, it was the popes who preached, financed, and organized the Crusades.

The social organization of Europe underwent profound changes as a result of the Crusades. Before leaving for the Holy Land, feudal lords would often free their serfs, either as an indication of religious zeal or for the more practical purpose of obtaining funds for the journey. The Church also freed thousands of serfs from their obligations once they took the crusader's vow. The resultant shortage of labor and the drift of peasants to the towns and cities led to the decline of serfdom. With the rise of commerce and industry in the towns, a new class of bourgeoisie (burghers, or residents of the bourg, town) came into existence.

As military expeditions, the Crusades were dismal failures, but they served to introduce new methods of warfare to the West. The crusaders borrowed methods of building fortifications from the Muslims, such as substituting the concentric castle for the more primitive fortresses of early feudal times. They learned how to employ various "fires" as missiles and how to use instruments of seige warfare. Impressed by Byzantine and Muslim methods of fighting, they borrowed from both.

There were also vital cultural results. Two centuries of migrations to and from the Muslim East could not but broaden the mental horizon of thousands of crusaders. Journeying from the cramped intellectual atmosphere of Western Europe, they came into contact with a civilization new to them. They were amazed by the magnificent cities, by the wealth, splendor, and luxury, and by the progress in art, science, and philosophy in the Byzantine and Muslim lands. Those who returned home transmitted new ideas they had acquired in intimate association with learned Muslims. The study of geography, history, mathematics, and literature was stimulated, and the old classical culture, kept alive by the Muslims, was transferred to the West.

The Crusades should be regarded not as the sole phenomenon of European history from 1100 to 1300, but as an important chapter in that development. Many results attributed to the Crusades might well have risen independent of the armed missions to the Holy Land. Change would have taken place anyhow. Feudalism was in decline, towns and cities were rising, trade and industry were extended, and there was an intellectual revival, all concurrent with the crusading expeditions.

Yet, the fact remains that with Urban's speech came a hastening of new forces on the horizon of Europe. In this sense the Crusades marked a major historical turning point.

MAGNA CARTA, 1215

"Why did not the barons ask for my kingdom also?"

FROM ancient times to the present there has been an unending search for that boundary mark at which individual freedom no longer impinges upon a workable social order. The old question remains, classic in its simplicity: does freedom of speech mean the right of any man, on impulse and just because he wants to do it, to yell "Fire!" in a crowded theatre?

In the long search for freedom the Magna Carta remains one of the most important documents in human development. In the words of Bishop Stubbs, the whole of the constitutional history of England is one long commentary on the Great Charter. This was a turning point in government — from this time on Magna Carta was the foundation for all future resistance to the evils of misgovernment. The basis of English liberties, it set a standard for the world.

Magna Carta contained nothing that was really new. It gave an admirable summary of the fundamental principles of government as they had existed in England until the early thirteenth century. Historians now recognize that its compilers were little concerned with the liberties of the common people; the men who drew up Magna Carta were just seeking to maintain their own rights. Some scholars even call it reactionary, "a very feudal document," because it was designed to protect the rights only of the nobility by binding the king to feudal law and custom.

However, the supreme importance of Magna Carta lies in the legal interpretations made of it in succeeding centuries — based on the assumption that *the king must keep the law.* Later, the knights and burgesses, who were growing in influence and importance, were to demand for themselves those rights and privileges specified for the nobility by the Magna Carta. Moreover, the doctrine of the uniformity of law had important advantages. Rightly or wrongly, the Magna Carta was interpreted as a prop for free government. Opponents of royal absolutism always invoked it as the keystone of liberty.

Englishmen regard the reign of King John (1199—1216) as probably the worst in their history. They look upon that monarch as one of the most unworthy sovereigns who ever occupied the throne. Throughout his life he revealed a quarrelsome nature, aggressive hostility, and childish insolence.

Even a limited recital reveals the quality of this contemptible monarch. Before he came to the throne, he joined with his brother Richard and the French king, Philip Augustus, in the conspiracy of 1189 against his own father, a plot which broke the heart of the elderly Henry II. After he became king, he drove a nobleman, William de Braose, into exile, and allowed his victim's wife and son to starve to death, because they were aware that John himself had murdered his own nephew.

John inherited great difficulties, but he made them worse. His reign was an era of humiliation. He surrendered to Rome, when Innocent III took England away from him and returned it to him as a personal fief of the papacy. Allied with the Emperor Otto IV and the Count of Flanders, John had to accept a bitter defeat at the battle of Bouvines from Philip Augustus of France.

Worst of all were John's heavy taxes and illegal extortions of money from the people. Because his expenses were heavy, particularly by reason of his wars in France, he devised all kinds of schemes to squeeze money from his subjects. He increased land taxes, almost doubled scutage (payments in lieu of military service), imposed excessive fines, confiscated property, and resurrected many old feudal levies and rights. The result of such high-handed measures was that all classes of Englishmen, including barons, clergy, and commons, were driven to protest.

The leadership against John fell to those who hated him most — the barons. More and more he began to levy fines on those who failed to accompany him on his campaigns. Because he distrusted his barons, John relied on mercenaries, whom he rewarded with important positions. The mercenaries, in turn, cared little for the welfare of their shires — they were concerned only for the monarch's interests, — and their own.

The circumstances surrounding the winning of the Charter were described by Roger of Wendover, a monk of the monastery of St. Alban's in Hertfordshire. His account begins with the meeting of the barons at Bury St. Edmunds in Suffolk in November 1214, and describes the granting of the Charter at Runnymede, June 15, 1215.

The earls and barons assembled at Bury St. Edmunds under the pretense of making a religious pilgrimage. Here in secret they discussed the charter of King Henry I, granted at his coronation in 1100, which contained a renunciation of the evil practices of William the Conqueror and William Rufus. The charter contained certain liberties and laws granted to the Church as well as to the nobles of the kingdom. The earls and barons swore on the great altar at Bury St. Edmunds that, if

John refused to grant these liberties and laws, they would withdraw their allegiance and make war on him. It was unanimously agreed that after Christmas 1214 they should all go together to the monarch and demand confirmation of their old liberties. Meanwhile, they would provide themselves with horses and arms.

In late December 1214 King John took residence at the New Temple in London. The nobles who had taken part in the secret conference came to the monarch in gay military array, and demanded confirmation of the liberties already granted them. Noting the bold tones of the petitioners, John feared an attack on his person. He replied that their demands were a matter of importance and difficulty; he, therefore, asked a truce until the end of Easter. After deliberation, he added, he might be able to satisfy them as well as retain the dignity of the Crown. He appointed some churchmen, including the Archbishop of Canterbury, as his sureties. Satisfied for the time being, the nobles returned to their homes.

Frightened by this incident, John demanded that all the nobles of England once again swear fealty to him. He also took a vow to go on a crusade, undoubtedly to obtain the personal protection which the sanctity of the vow carried with it.

In Easter week, the dissident barons, by this time joined by virtually all the nobility of England, assembled at Stamford. The host included some 2,000 knights, including horse-soldiers, attendants, and foot-soldiers. From Oxford the king sent delegates to inquire what were the laws and liberties which the nobles demanded. The barons sent back a paper containing a detailed list of the ancient laws and customs of the kingdom. Unless their rights were immediately granted, they would take possession of the king's fortresses.

When John received this message, he reacted indignantly: "Why, amongst these unjust demands, do not the barons ask for my kingdom also? Their demands are vain and visionary, and are unsupported by any plea of reason whatever." He angrily declared that he would never grant them such liberties as would render him their slave.

When the barons heard what John had said, they appointed Robert fitz Walter commander of their armies, gave him the new title of "Marshal of the Army of God and the Holy Church," and marched on Northampton in central England to lay siege to the castle there. For fifteen days they made no progress, primarily because they lacked *petrariae,* engines for hurling stones. They proceeded in confusion to the castle of Bedford. Meanwhile, a message came from London telling them to go there at once.

Marching the whole night, the nobles arrived in London early in the morning of May 24 to find the gates open. They entered the city without incident while the inhabitants were at church. The time was favorable: the rich citizens were on their side, and the poor were afraid to speak against them. From London the nobles sent letters throughout the country to earls, barons, and knights who were still faithful to the king. "Abandon the monarch who had made war against his barons!" "Stand firm and fight for your rights and for peace!" "If you refuse, you will be attacked as open enemies!" The greater part of those receiving the messages joined the dissident barons and set out for London.

King John realized to his dismay that he was deserted by almost all the nobles. Only seven knights stayed with him. Alarmed that the barons would attack his castles and reduce them to rubble, he tried further delaying tactics. He pretended to make peace, sending messengers to inform the barons that he would willingly grant them the laws and liberties they demanded. What would be a suitable day and place to meet? The barons joyfully suggested June 15 at Runnymede-on-the-Thames on a field lying between Staines and Windsor. King and nobles met that day, each stationed at some distance from the other. Then came long discussions about terms of peace.

John finally granted the demanded laws and liberties. Roger of Wendover told the story in his *Flowers of History:* [1]

> King John, when he saw that he was deserted by almost all, so that out of his regal superabundance of followers he scarcely retained seven knights, was much alarmed lest the barons would attack his castles and reduce them without difficulty, as they would find no obstacle to their so doing; and he deceitfully pretended to make peace for a time with the aforesaid barons, and sent William Marshal earl of Pembroke, with other trustworthy messengers, to them, and told them that, for the sake of peace, and for the exaltation and honor of the kingdom, he would willingly grant them the laws and liberties they required; he also sent word to the barons by these same messengers, to appoint a fitting day and place to meet and carry all these matters into effect. The king's messengers then came in all haste to London, and without deceit reported to the barons all that had been deceitfully imposed on them; they in their great joy appointed the fifteenth of June for the king to meet them, at a field lying between Staines and Windsor. Accordingly, at the time and place pre-agreed on, the king and nobles came to the appointed conference, and when each party had stationed themselves apart from the other, they began a long discussion about terms of peace and the aforesaid liberties. . . . At length, after various points on both sides had been discussed, King John, seeing that he was inferior in strength to the barons, without raising any difficulty, granted the underwritten laws and liberties, and confirmed them by his charter. . . .

The Charter was a lengthy document, of which only a few of the important clauses are given here in condensed form:

> 1. That the Church of England shall be free, and have her whole rights, and her liberties inviolable.
> 2. We also have granted to all the freemen of our kingdom, for us and for our heirs forever, all the underwritten liberties, to be had and holden by them and their heirs, of us and our heirs forever.
> 12. No scutage [from *scutum,* "shield," payment made to the king by persons who owed military service but preferred to give money instead] shall be imposed in our kingdom unless by the general council of our kingdom.

---

[1] Roger of Wendover, *Flowers of History,* trans. J. A. Giles (London, 1849), II, 308–309.

14. For the holding of a General Council of the kingdom we shall cause to be summoned the archbishops, bishops, abbots, earls, and greater barons of the realm, singly by our letters.

36. Nothing from henceforth shall be given or taken for a writ of inquisition of life or limb, but it shall be granted freely, and not denied [an important legal enactment for the purpose of preventing prolonged imprisonment without trial of persons accused of serious crimes].

40. We will sell to no man, we will not deny to any man, either justice or right.

41. All merchants shall have safe and secure conduct to go out of, and to come into, England.

51. As soon as peace is restored, we will send out of the kingdom all foreign knights, cross-bowmen, and stipendiaries, who are come with horses and arms to the molestation of our people. [All Englishmen resented John's importation of foreign mercenaries.]

61. We do give and grant our subjects the underwritten security, namely, that the barons may choose five and twenty barons of the kingdom to hold, observe, and cause to be observed, the peace and liberties we have granted them, and by this our present Charter confirmed.

63. It is also sworn, as well on our part as on the part of the barons, that all the things aforesaid shall be observed in good faith, and without evil duplicity.

Given under our hand, in the presence of the witnesses above named, and many others, in the meadow called Runnymede, between Windsor and Staines, the 15th day of June, in the 17th year of our reign.

King John did not "sign" the Charter after the fashion of modern sovereigns. There is no evidence that he could write — he agreed to the terms merely by affixing his seal to the paper. Legend has it that he was so humiliated and angered by the necessity of agreeing to the terms that he awaited until the barons left, threw himself on the floor of his tent, and in rage began to chew the carpet.

Magna Carta set in motion the demand for liberty of the individual, a struggle in which Englishmen have played a long and honorable part. A precedent was set in 1215 for the limitation of monarchical power, a turning point in the continuing efforts to define the nature of the power structure. It remains of import today in a society beset by political confrontation, riots, and confusion of dissent with anarchy. How to balance liberty with authority remains the key problem of the democratic world.

THE INVENTION OF PRINTING, c. 1445

"Germany has both books and documents."

VICTOR HUGO called it the greatest invention of all time. It facilitated the spread of knowledge by introducing a technique for producing books by the hundreds and thousands instead of single copies painfully copied by hand. Knowledge could now be communicated on a large scale, and texts could be duplicated inexpensively. Cheap books and pamphlets enabled the men of the Renaissance to extend their influence among the masses. The first break with ecclesiastical authority occurred in Northern Europe, where the printing press was first introduced.

The art of printing originated in Asia. Block printing was probably used in Korea and Japan as early as the eighth century A.D. This method utilized characters and pictures carved by hand on the face of wooden blocks; after ink was applied, an impression was made on parchment or papyrus. An identical procedure produced playing cards and paper money. The oldest known book printed from blocks, discovered in 1900 in the Chinese province of Kansu, bears this statement: "Printed on May 11, 868, by Wang Chieh, for free general distribution, in order in deep reverence to perpetuate the memory of his parents."

The first printing from movable type was done by a Chinese craftsman, Pi Sheng, about 1040 A.D. His technique used movable type made of baked clay or porcelain. There was a weakness, however, in the multiplicity of characters — there were many thousands of them — which called for far too many different pieces of type. It was far easier to print from wooden blocks. Hence the Chinese reverted to block type and played no role in the development of movable type.

Block printing spread beyond China into areas throughout the Far East, and eventually to Western Europe. Exactly how it was introduced into Western Europe is not clear. Tradition has it that Marco Polo brought back a printing block on his return from the Far East in 1295. Other historians say that missionaries borrowed the technique from Asia. Still others suggest that it became known through the use of Chinese playing cards. Whatever the explanation, it is clear that block printing was used in Western Europe, especially for religious subjects, as early as the fourteenth century. A print dated 1423 pictures St. Christopher fording a stream with the child Jesus on his shoulder. The caption reads:

> Each day that thou the likeness of St. Christopher
>   shall see
> That day no frightful form of death shall make an
>   end of thee.

As late as the middle of the fourteenth century, all books in Western Europe were copied entirely by hand. Shortly afterward, the practice of printing from engraved blocks of wood was introduced. The crude "block books" and "block pamphlets" represented an advance over the old methods of copying by pen.

The type mold, which allowed separate types to be cast in quantity, made the printed book the successful rival of the manuscript. This epoch-making "invention," probably the work of a German, Johann Gutenberg of Mayence (c.1398–1468), was made available to Europeans at some time during the decade after 1440. About 1428 Gutenberg settled in Strassburg, where he worked on block printing and invented a special press for multiplying impressions. From 1444 to 1450 he was occupied in Mayence in perfecting his art. In the latter year he entered into a partnership with a rich burgher named Faust or Fust, who lent him the money to set up a printing press. The partnership was finally dissolved when Faust sued Gutenberg to recover his money. As a result of the verdict Faust obtained the press.

Whether or not Gutenberg invented printing from movable type has been the subject of considerable controversy. Most historians give Gutenberg credit, but others say that the honor belongs to Laurenz Janzoon, surnamed Coster, of Haarlem. It is claimed that twenty years before Gutenberg, Coster had the idea of carving out characters from cubes of wood, and that he used these to form inscriptions to accompany engravings. Later on he used metal instead of wood. It is further claimed that a dishonest employee stole some of Coster's apparatus, took it to Mayence, and there set up a printing business, taking in Gutenberg as a partner. The identity of the real inventor has never been ascertained.

Claims are made for many countries. The mystery stimulated this poem:

> Holland has books but no documents,
> France has documents but no books;
> Italy has neither books nor documents;
> Germany has both books and documents.

The following passage, from the *Chronicles of Cologne* (1499), contains one of the very few contemporary references to the invention of the printing press:

> The eternal God has out of his unfathomable wisdom brought into existence the laudable art, by which men now print books, and multiply them so greatly that every man may for himself read or hear read the way of salvation . . . .
>
> Item — this most valuable art aforesaid is found first of all in Germany at Mayence on the Rhine. And it is a great honor for the German nation that such ingenious men are there to be found. And this came to pass about the year of our Lord 1440 and from thence forward until 1450 is written the art was investigated and what belongs to it. And in the year of our Lord which is written 1450, there was a Golden year and men began to print and the first book that they printed was the Bible in Latin, and it was printed in a large character, such as the character with which Missal Books are now printed.
>
> Item — although the art is found at Mayence as aforesaid in the manner as it is now generally used, yet the first prefiguration is found in Holland out of the Donatuses which were in that very [country] printed before that time. And from and out of them was taken the beginning of the aforesaid art. And it is found much more masterly and subtilely [sic] than that same manner was and the longer [it was practiced] the more skillful it became . . . . The first inventor of printing was a burgher at Mainz, and he was born at Strassburg, and named Johann Gutenberg. Item from Mayence as aforesaid art came first of all to Cologne, then to Strassburg, and thereafter to Venice. The beginning and development of the aforesaid art was told me by word of mouth by the honorable man Master Ulrich Zell of Hanau, Anno 1490, a printer at Cologne by whome the aforesaid art came to Cologne.

Although he was not successful commercially, Gutenberg had some important books associated with his name, including the Latin Mazarin or 42-line Bible of 1452-1455; the 36-line Bible, 1457-1459; and the *Catholicon*, 1460. For the rest of his life Gutenberg suffered from financial troubles. After publishing the *Catholicon*, he printed a papal bull promulgated by Pope Pius II. Then he retired, his health weakened by years of struggle and disappointment. In 1465 Adolf of Nassau, Archbishop of Mayence, made him an honorary member of his staff, and awarded him a small pension. He died in 1468. One writer described the meaning of his life: "There is no other instance in modern history, excepting perhaps Shakespeare, of a man who did so much and said so little about it."

The name of Gutenberg was obscured by the fog of jealousy. He was damned by scribes who earned a livelihood by copying manuscripts. Parisian copyists for a time succeeded in halting the use of printing presses altogether, but it was a hopeless rebellion against progress. In 1470 there were 6,000 scribes engaged in copying manuscripts, but within a few years their profession had almost disappeared. Printing with movable type spread with incredible speed through Europe and the world.

An adequate supply of paper had come to Europe from factories in the Islamic countries where the making of paper from wood fibers and old rags was a long-established industry. Germans were responsible for the diffusion of printing throughout Europe. Leipzig, Cologne, Nuremberg, Augsburg, Wittenberg, and Frankfort-on-Main took the lead in printing and publishing books. Within a few decades, the printing press was brought to Italy, where it played an important role in the later Renaissance. By the end of the fifteenth century, seventy-three Italian cities had printing presses, which produced over 4,100 editions, chiefly of the classics.

The new technique gained momentum. By 1500, printing presses were used in thirteen European countries. Publishers began issuing classical works as well as vernacular literature. There were accurate texts devoted to the odes of Horace, the orations of Cicero, and the verse of Virgil. Printed editions of the works of Aristotle appeared. Records show that sixteen works by Erasmus were published. The clergy, wealthy burghers, and students all purchased books – regarded as a status symbol. Collectors began to boast of their large libraries.

There were some diehards. Frederick Montefeltro, Duke of Urbino, declared that he would be ashamed to own a printed book and would not have one in his library. Trithemius, Abbot of Spanheim, was convinced that paper could not endure: "A work written on parchment can be preserved for a thousand years, while it is probable that no volume printed on paper will last for more than two centuries." But these were exceptional voices. Printing from movable type had come to stay.

The art of printing in England deserves special mention. In other countries the pioneers were wandering German craftsmen who insisted on working in Latin. England's pioneer printer was William Caxton (c. 1422–1491), who preferred to use his own language. Born in Kent, Caxton as a young man served as an apprentice to a rich silk mercer. For the next thirty years he lived in Bruges in what is today Belgium, where he became governor of a colony of English merchants known as "the English nation." He learned the art of printing at Cologne, and on returning to his home at Bruges he set up his own press, on which he printed several treatises.

Caxton then returned to England to live at Westminster, where he established his own press at the Red Pale in the Almonry. The first known piece of printing issued from the Caxton Press was a papal indulgence issued by Abbé Sant on December 13, 1476. From this time and for fifteen years until his death, Caxton continued his printing activities, producing about a hundred volumes, amounting to 18,000 pages, apparently with little skilled help. His *Dictes or Sayenges of the Phylosophers*, printed in 1477, was the first book printed in England to bear a date. His services to typography were considerable, including type faces of a design that was neither Gothic nor Roman.

The invention of printing was decisive for the humanist world of the early sixteenth century. From approximately 1400 to 1600, at the midway point between medieval scholasticism and modern science, a revival of learning occurred to which is given the name "humanism." It was characterized by two qualities:

regard for man as man, not merely as a candidate for salvation, and interest in the revival and re-evaluation of Greek and Roman literature.

Classical literature had been popular among scholars throughout most of the Middle Ages, chiefly because it provided an excellent model for style. It was pagan in outlook, surrounded with mysticism and allegory, and fused with Christian theology. The humanists began to read the classics for meaning as well as for form and style. Unlike medieval scholastics, the humanists were not content to use Aristotle and other pagan writers as supports for Christian theology, or to justify faith by reason. On the contrary, they tried to view each classical work as a whole, and to interpret it in terms of its own era.

Humanism sparked a great treasure hunt. Under the impulse of this revived interest in ancient learning, scholars ransacked the libraries of Europe, and copied, recopied, edited, criticized, and translated all the works of the obscure, as well as the great pagan writers. Grammars and dictionaries necessary for this great scholarly activity appeared by the dozens. Learning became fashionable, and its influence pervaded all society. For generations reared on decadent scholasticism and stereotyped theology, the new learning turned out to be an intellectual rebirth.

The progress of humanism in France was halted temporarily by scholars at the University of Paris, who adhered rigidly to the old scholasticism. The new learning was more powerful, however, than the prestige of even so venerable an institution as the university. As in Germany and England, a long line of humanist scholars built up a body of classical knowledge. The central figure among the great French scholars was the Franciscan monk François Rabelais (c. 1495–1553), a physician and a boisterous critic. In his printed works he expressed the same desire for social reform that motivated the similar writings of Erasmus and Sir Thomas More. Variously labeled "the great jester of France," "a comic Homer," and "an obscene jester," Rabelais was an outstanding example of the humanist temper brought to the public by the printing press.

Much of Rabelais's work was sheer buffoonery, full of unrestrained hilarity. He mocked almost everything opposed to naturalness and what he saw as human qualities. "For laughter is the proper occupation of man." But he was most serious on the invention of printing, which to him distinguished his day from that of the Greeks. Rabelais had Gargantua write the following to Pantraguel:

> Now it is that the minds of men are qualified with all manner of discipline, and the old sciences revived which for many ages were extinct. Now it is that the learned languages are to their pristine purity restored, viz., Greek, without which a man may be ashamed to account himself a scholar, Hebrew, Arabic, Chaldaean, and Latin. Printing likewise is now in use, so elegant and so correct that better cannot be imagined, although it was found out but in my time by divine inspiration, as by a diabolical suggestion on the other side was the invention of ordnance. All the world is full of knowing men, of most learned schoolmasters, and vast libraries; and it appears to me as a truth, that neither in Plato's time, nor Cicero's nor Papinian's, there was ever such convenience for studying as we

see at this day there is. Nor must any adventurer henceforward come in public, or present himself in company, that hath not been pretty well polished in the shop of Minerva. I see robbers, hangmen, freebooters, tapsters, ostlers, and such like, of the very rubbish of the people, more learned now than the doctors and preachers were in my time.

Rabelais was concerned because "the very rubbish of the people" were more learned now "than the doctors and preachers" — thanks to the printing press. But this was Rabelaisian tongue-in-cheek talk. He knew well that the printing press meant a turning point in the history of communication.

Rabelais was expressing a good-natured view of a magnificent step in man's progress. Thomas Carlyle, in his heavy-handed and ponderous prose, pronounced a more serious judgment in *Sartor Resartus:*

He who first shortened the labor of Copyists by device of *Movable Types* was disbanding hired Armies and cashiering most Kings and Senates and creating a whole new Democratic world: he had invented the Art of printing.

Carlyle was right; communication made possible by printing contributed to the rise of modern democracies because it made for an informed citizenry.

One technical refinement followed another until tons of paper flowed through the printing presses. In 1814 the London *Times* announced with pride the use of the steam press to speed the printing process. Then followed the rotary press, typesetting, intaglio printing, and printed electronic circuits. Gutenberg would have been amazed by the flowering of his simple idea.

DISCOVERY OF AMERICA BY CHRISTOPHER COLUMBUS, 1492

"Come! Come! and see the man from heaven!"

A CHANGE of course in the mainstream of Western civilization came with the expansion of Europe at the dawn of the modern era. During ancient and medieval times the Mediterranean Sea was the fulcrum of Western trade and culture. But the modern age saw the center of gravity move from the Mediterranean area to the oceans of the world — first around the coast line of Africa to the Far East, and then across the Atlantic to the New World. Within several centuries Europeans brought most of the world under their control, and left traces of their languages, traditions, customs, ideals, and religion everywhere. What is known today as the modern world is in a very real sense the extension of European civilization.

Behind this phenomenon, as is customary in history, was a long development. The Crusades were unsuccessful in wresting the Holy Sepulcher from the Muslims, but they did help prepare Western Europe for overseas expansion. Crusaders returning from the Holy Land brought back tales of wealth and luxury — enough to stimulate new knowledge and new demands.

In the early fourteenth century most of Mediterranean commerce was controlled by Italian city-states, notably Venice, Genoa, and Florence. Northern commerce around the Baltic and North Seas was dominated by merchants of the Hanseatic League. Both monopolies — the Italian and the German — functioned well, and held rigid control. Each traded with the other through the Alpine passes. But their time of economic domination was coming to an end.

Advances in geographical knowledge helped prepare the way for expansion. During most of the Middle Ages, scholars regarded the earth as a flat disk, with

Jerusalem at its center. There were vague maps which showed islands off the Western coasts of Europe, but mariners were reluctant to venture far out because of the supposed existence of terrible sea monsters.

In the thirteenth century bold Franciscan friars journeyed to the Far East to convert the Mongol emperors and their people to Christianity. They were unsuccesful in this task, nor did they add much to the existing geographical knowledge. The brothers Nicolo and Maffeo Polo, natives of Venice, traveled to the land of Cathay in the latter part of the thirteenth century. Nicolo's son, the well-known Marco Polo, gave an astonishing account of the riches and splendor of the Far Orient, and with it aroused the imagination of European merchants and adventurers.

The Muslims not only inherited the geographical knowledge of the Greeks and Romans, but also learned much themselves about the geography of Africa, India, and China. They, too, stimulated other explorers to find and exploit the fabulous treasures of distant lands.

Improvements in knowledge of geography and navigation gave impulse to exploration. By the fifteenth century the magnetic compass (probably introduced from China) was in general use among Mediterranean mariners. Now they dared to leave the sight of land, and to sail on starless nights. They used the astrolabe, which measured the altitude of the sun, to reckon latitude at sea, although a satisfactory method of determining longitude was not to be discovered until the eighteenth century. The hourglass, the minute glass, and the sundial were basic navigation instruments. The *portolani*, or compass charts of the coasts, were also helpful. With a growing knowledge of astronomy winds and currents, mariners could venture with some degree of confidence into the vast oceans.

Maritime architecture also advanced. Caravels, large ships carrying two or three masts with triangular sails, were fairly well equipped for hazardous conditions in the open seas. The diffusion of geographical and maritime knowledge was facilitated by the invention of the printing press by Gutenberg. Circulation of the latest sailing charts and maps contributed to an ever-increasing maritime activity.

Portugal, leader in the discovery of new trade routes, was a small country, occupying some 35,000 square miles on the west side of the Iberian peninsula. During Roman and early medieval periods, Portugal was merely an obscure border section of Spain, and shared its history. Between 1095 and 1279 a Portuguese kingdom was established, and extended until it reached its present limits. Between 1279 and 1415 the monarchy was gradually consolidated, despite opposition from nobility, Church, and the kingdom of Castile. Portugal became one of the most unified nations in Europe. The Portuguese, living on the western seaboard of Europe where excellent harbors were available, began where the Arab explorers had left off, and ventured into the Atlantic. They fashioned the first colonial empire in modern times — an empire reaching from Brazil to the East Indies.

The elements favoring the expansion of Portugal were brilliantly co-ordinated by Prince Henry of Portugal (surnamed the Navigator; 1394—1460), whose father, John I, had been successful in unifying his country at the expense of Castilians and

Moors in Morocco. In 1415, while still a young man, Henry took part in the storming of Ceuta, the Gibraltar of Africa, which was taken from the Moors. Thereafter, he regarded as his mission the continuance of crusades against the Moors. His expeditionary activities along the coast line of Africa were designed to gather information about the enemy. Furthermore, he was intrigued by the possibility of establishing contact with a legendary Christian ruler, Prester John, who was said to have established a Christian kingdom in the Far East.

Prince Henry was not insensitive to the possibilities of trade opened by his explorers, nor to the desirability of obtaining gold and slaves. He sent expeditions southward along the west coast of Africa; his captains reached the Madeiras and the Azores in the Atlantic Ocean.

Returning in 1419 from an expedition in Morocco, Prince Henry settled in Sagres, known as The Infante's Town (Villa do Iffante), which later became a naval arsenal and the favorite center of court life. He gathered around his person an outstanding group of captains, pilots, and maritime scientists, including the famed cartographers Master Jacome of Majorca and Master Peter, and a number of Arab and Jewish mathematicians. Henry trained his captains in the art of navigation and in the making of maps and nautical instruments. In the nearby port of Lagos, he supervised the construction of large caravels which left Portugal under his flag. From 1444 to 1446 more than thirty ships sailed to Guinea on his orders. He himself never accompanied his captains on their explorations of Africa and the Atlantic, but his patient planning led to one success after another, and to the emergence of Portugal as a prosperous maritime power.

Christopher Columbus (c. 1451–1506), who made the discovery of America for Spain, was born in the neighborhood of Genoa. He went to sea at the age of fourteen, settled at Lisbon, married the daughter of one of Prince Henry's captains, and served for some years under the Portuguese crown. It is not certain whether his purpose was to reach the East Indies and Cathay by sailing west, or whether he wanted to discover new islands in the Atlantic for his sponsors. At any rate, he appealed for financial backing to several persons, all of whom rejected his proposals as fantastic. Finally, on April 17, 1492, he was commissioned by Ferdinand and Isabella to sail westward and test his theory that he could reach the fabulous wealth of Asia.

On August 3, 1492, Columbus set out from the town of Palos with one ship of 100 tons, the *Santa Maria*, and two caravels, the *Pinta* of 50 tons and the *Nina* of 40 tons. His first stop was the Canary Islands, from which on September 6 the expedition sailed westward. From the beginning Columbus was faced with insubordination and near mutiny among his crews, who were reduced to terror by rumored variations of the magnetic needle. On October 12 an island was sighted, and named San Salvador. The expedition cruised in the vicinity, discovering Cuba and Hispaniola (Haiti). The *Santa Maria*, which went aground on Hispaniola, was abandoned there. Columbus returned to Spain in the remaining two caravels to receive a tremendous welcome.

While optimistic about the wealth of the newly opened lands, Columbus had not the least idea that he had discovered a New World. These lands, he said, were merely an extension of Asia. He believed that only a channel separated the West Indies from "The Golden Chersonese of Ptolemy" (the Malay Peninsula) and that "it was no farther from Panama to the Ganges than from Pisa to Genoa." To the end of his life, as Samuel Eliot Morison, his biographer, has pointed out, Columbus remained "absolutely and completely wrong." In addition to his faults as a geographer, Columbus was a wretched administrator; under his regime the natives of Hispaniola were exploited in the quest for gold.

Some writers have tried to explode the tradition that Columbus discovered America. Indeed, Columbus was probably not the first to reach the New World. There are those who say that the Phoenicians who circumnavigated Africa may have reached South America about 1000 B.C. It is also believed that Leif Ericsson crossed the Atlantic at the beginning of the eleventh century. Columbus himself reported on his third voyage the presence of Negroes in lands he had visited. It is probable that the natives of Guinea crossed over from Africa in canoes from time to time. But the Admiral was the important pioneer in the Age of Discovery — his accounts set in motion a long procession of explorers, soldiers, and priests.

Columbus reported wonders to a credulous world in a letter to the Marrano (convert from Judaism) Luis de Santangel, treasurer of Spanish Aragon and a backer of his expedition. This announcement of the exploration of the West Indies, written on his return from his first expedition, became a best seller, and ran through a dozen editions within a few years.

The original letter to Santangel is lost, but it was the first of Columbus's letters to be set in type and it was printed in the original Spanish at Barcelona shortly after its receipt. Only one copy is known to exist and that is in the possession of the New York Public Library. It is reprinted here:

Sir:

Believing that you will rejoice at the glorious success that our Lord has granted me in my voyage, I write this to tell you how in thirty-three days I reached the Indies with the fleet which the most illustrious King and Queen, our Sovereigns, gave me, where I discovered a great many thickly-populated islands. Without meeting resistance, I have taken possession of them all for their Highnesses by issuing proclamation and by unfurling the royal standard.

To the first island I discovered I gave the name of San Salvador[1] in remembrance of His High Majesty, who had marvellously brought all this to pass. The Indians call it Guanahan. The second I named the Island of Santa Maria de Concepcion;[2] the third, Fernandina;[3] the fourth Isabella;[4] the fifth, Juana;[5]

---

[1] Watling Island.

[2] Rum Cay.   [3] Lond Island.   [4] Crooked Island.   [5] Cuba.

and thus to each I gave a new name. When I reached Juana, I followed its coast to the westward, and found it so large that I thought it must be the mainland — the province of Cathay; and, as I found neither towns nor villages on the seacoast, save for a few hamlets, where it was impossible to speak to the people because they all took flight instantly, I continued on the same route, thinking I could not fail to light upon some great cities or towns. At length, after traversing many leagues and finding nothing new, and observing that the coast was leading me northward (which I wished to avoid, because winter had already set in and it was my intention to head for the south; and because, moreover, the winds were contrary), I resolved not to wait for a change in the weather, but returned to a certain harbor whence I sent two men ashore to ascertain whether there was any king or large cities in that region. They explored for three days, and found countless small hamlets with numberless inhabitants, but with no kind of government. They therefore returned.

In the meantime I had learned from some other Indians I had already taken that this land was without question an island. Accordingly, I followed the coast eastward for a distance of one hundred and seven leagues, where it ended in a cape. From that point I saw another isle to the eastward at eighteen leagues distance, to which I gave the name of Hispaniola. [6] Thither I went, and followed its northern coast to the eastward (just as I had done in Juana), one hundred and seventy-eight leagues [7] due east.

This island, like all the others, is extraordinarily large. It has many ports excelling any in Christendom. The lands are high, with numerous mountains and peaks incomparably higher than on the island of Cetefrey. They are all most beautiful, of a thousand different shapes, accessible, and covered with an endless variety of trees of such great height that they seem to reach the sky. I am told that they never lose their foliage. They appeared as green and luxuriant as trees are in Spain in the month of May. Some were in bloom, others bearing fruit, and still others varied according to their nature. The nightingale and other small birds of a thousand different kinds were singing; and that, in November, the month when I was there. There were palm trees of six or eight kinds, wonderful in their beautiful variety. The same holds for all the other trees and fruits and grasses. Trees, plants, or fruits filled us with admiration. There are wonderful pine groves, and very extensive plains. There is also honey, many kinds of birds, and a great variety of fruits. In the interior there are many mines of metals and innumerable people.

Hispaniola is, indeed, a wonder. Its mountains and plains, its meadows and fields, are so rich and fertile for planting and for pasturage, and for building towns and villages. Its harbors are incredibly fine, and the number and size and magnificence of its rivers, most of which bear gold, surpass anything that could be believed by any who had not seen them. The trees, fruits, and grasses differ widely from those in Juana. In this island there are many spices and extensive mines of gold and other metals. The inhabitants, both men and women, of this and all the other islands I have discovered or gained intelligence of, go as naked

---

[6] Or San Domingo.   [7] Actually 188 leagues.

as they were born, with the exception that some of the women cover one part only with a single leaf of grass or with a piece of cotton, made for that purpose. They have neither iron nor steel nor weapons, nor are they competent to use them; not that they are not well-formed and of handsome stature, but because they are extraordinarily timid. Their only arms are sticks of cane, cut in the seeding time, to which they fasten small sharpened sticks, and even these they dare not use. On several occasions I have sent two or three men ashore to some villages to converse with them, and the natives have come out in countless numbers, but, as soon as they saw our men approach, would flee with such haste that a father would not even stop to protect his son; and this, not because any harm had been done to any of them, for, from the first, wherever I went and had speech with them, I gave them of all that I had, such as cloth and many other things, without receiving anything in return, but they are, as I have described, incurably timid.

It is true that, when they are reassured and have thrown off this fear, they are guileless and so generous of all they have that no one would believe it who had not seen it. They never refuse anything that is asked for. On the contrary, they even offer it themselves, and exhibit so much loving kindness that they would give their very hearts. Whether it be something of value or of little worth that is offered them, they are content. I forbade that worthless things, such as bits of broken bowls, pieces of glass, and ends of straps, be given to them; although, when they succeeded in obtaining them, they thought they possessed the finest jewel in the world. One sailor was found to have received for a leather strap a piece of gold weighing two and a half castellanos, [8] and others much more for objects of far less value. For new blancas [9] they would give all they had, were it two or three castellanos of gold or an arroba [10] or two of spun cotton. Even bits of broken hoops of wine casks they accepted, and gave, like fools, all that they possessed in return. This seemed wrong to me, and I forbade it. I gave away a thousand good and pretty articles which I had brought with me in order to win their affection, to induce them to become Christians, and to love and serve their Highnesses and the whole Spanish nation, and to help us by giving us things of which we stand in need, but which they possess in abundance.

They have no religion, and are not idolators, but believe that all power and goodness are in heaven. They are firmly convinced that I, with my ships and men, came from heaven, and, in this belief, received me at every place at which I touched, after they had overcome their apprehension. This does not spring from ignorance, for they are very intelligent, and navigate all these seas and relate everything to us astonishingly well; but they have never seen men with clothes on, nor vessels like ours.

On my reaching the Indies, I took by force, in the first island I discovered, some of these natives, that they might learn our language and give me information in regard to what existed in these parts; and it so happened that they soon understood us and we them, either by words or signs, and they have been very

---

[8] An old Spanish coin, equal to the fiftieth part of a mark of gold.

[9] Small copper coins, equal to about a quarter of a farthing.   [10] One arroba weighs 25 lbs.

serviceable to us. They are still with me, and, from repeated conversations that I have had with them, I find that they still believe that I come from heaven. They were the first to declare this wherever I went, and the others ran from house to house and to the neighboring villages, crying out,

"Come! Come! and see the man from heaven!"

Then all, both men and women, once reassured about us, came, both small and great, and brought us something to eat and drink, which they gave us with extraordinary kindness.

They have in all these islands very many canoes like our rowboats: some larger, some smaller, but most of them larger than a barge of eighteen seats. They are not so wide, because they are made of one single piece of timber, but a barge could not keep up with them in rowing, because they go with incredible speed, and with these canoes they navigate among these islands (which are innumerable) and carry on their commerce. I have seen some of these canoes with seventy and eighty men, each with his oar.

In all these islands I observed little difference in the appearance of the inhabitants, nor in their manners nor language, except that they all understood each other, which is very singular, and leads me to hope that their Highnesses will take means for their conversion to our holy faith, toward which they are very well disposed.

I have already said how I had gone one hundred and seven leagues in following the seacoast of Juana in a straight line from west to east: and from that survey I can state that the island is larger than England and Scotland together, because, beyond these one hundred and seven leagues, there lie to the west two provinces which I have not yet visited, one of which is called Avan, where the people are born with a tail. These two provinces cannot be less in length from fifty to sixty leagues, from what can be learned from the Indians that I have with me, and who are acquainted with all these islands. The other, Hispaniola, has a greater circumference than all Spain, from Catalonia by the seacoast to Fuenterabia in Biscay, since on one of its four sides I have made one hundred and eighty-eight great leagues in a straight line from west to east. This is something to covet, and when found not to be lost sight of.

There was one large town in Hispaniola of which especially I took possession, situated in a locality well adapted for the working of the gold mines, and for all kinds of commerce, either with the mainland on this side, or with that beyond which is the land of the Great Khan, with which there will be vast commerce and great profit. To that city I gave the name of Villa de Navidad, and fortified it with a fortress, which by this time will be quite completed, and I have left in it a sufficient number of men with arms, artillery, and provisions to hold it for more than a year, as well as a barge and a master seaman skillful in the arts necessary for building others. I have struck up such friendly relations with the king of that country that he was proud to call me his brother and hold me as such. Even should he change his mind and wish to quarrel with my men, neither he nor his subjects know what arms are, but go naked, and are the most timid people in the world. The men I have left there could, unassisted, destroy the whole country, and will run no risk if they only know how to behave properly.

In all these islands the men seem to be satisfied with one wife, save for their chief or king, whom they allow twenty. The women appear to me to work harder than the men. I have not been able to ascertain whether they have any property of their own. It seemed to me that what one had was shared with the rest, particularly food. I have not found in those islands any monsters, as some expected; but, on the contrary, the people are very well formed, nor are they black, as in Guinea, but their hair is flowing, for they do not dwell where the sun's rays are too potent. It is true that the sun has very great power here, for the country is distant only twenty-six degrees from the equinoctial line. In the islands where there are high mountains, the cold this winter was very severe, but the people endure it, not only from being habituated to it, but with the aid of meat eaten with excessively hot spices.

As for savages, I found no trace of them, except at the second island as one approaches the Indies.[11] This is inhabited by a people regarded throughout these islands as extremely ferocious and eaters of human flesh. They possess many canoes, in which they visit all the Indian islands, and rob and plunder whatever they can. They are no worse looking than the others, except that they wear their hair long, like women, and use bows and arrows of the same cane, with a sharp stock at the end for want of iron, which they do not possess. Compared to these exceedingly cowardly people, they are truly ferocious. They are said to marry with the women of Matenino, [12] the first island one comes to en route from Spain to the Indies, and in which there are no men. These women employ themselves in no labor suitable to their sex; but use bows and arrows of cane like those previously described, and arm and cover themselves with plates of copper, of which they have a great quantity. Another island, I am told (larger than Hispaniola) boasts natives who have no hair and countless gold. I bring with me Indians taken from these different islands to testify to all these points.

Finally, and speaking only of what has taken place in this hurried voyage, their Highnesses will see that I can give them all the gold they require, if they, in turn, will give me a little assistance, spices, cotton (as much as their Highnesses shall command to be shipped), and mastic, which until now has only been found in Greece, in the island of Chios, and which the Signoria sells at its own price; as much lign aloes as their Highnesses shall command to be shipped, and as many slaves — all heathen — as they choose to send. I think I have found rhubarb and cinnamon. A thousand other things of value will be found by the men I have left behind, for I tarried at no point so long as the wind allowed me to proceed, except in the town of Navidad, which I left fortified and safe. Indeed, I might have accomplished much more had my vessels been in as good a condition as by rights they ought to have been.

Praised be the eternal mighty God, our Lord, Who gives to all who walk in His way victory over the seeming impossible; of which this voyage is signally an example, for, although others may have spoken or written about these countries, it was mere conjecture, as no one could say that he had seen them. As a result, those who heard listened the more, but regarded the matter more as a fable than

---

[11] Dominica.   [12] Martinique.

anything else. But our Redeemer hath granted this victory to our most illustrious King and Queen and to their kingdoms rendered famous by this glorious event. In this all Christendom should rejoice, celebrating the event with great festivities and solemn thanksgivings to the Holy Trinity, with fervent prayers for the high distinction that will accrue to them in turning so many nations to our holy faith, and for the temporal benefits, not only to Spain, but to all Christians. Therefore, I have set down briefly these happenings. Farewell.

Written on board the caravel, off the Canary Isles, on the 15th of February, 1493.

Yours to command,

THE ADMIRAL

Columbus announced the discovery of a new continent, but the honor of its name fell to a boastful liar and a phony navigator. Ralph Waldo Emerson voiced a common complaint: "Strange that broad America must wear the name of a thief! Amerigo Vespucci, the pickle-dealer at Seville, who went out in 1499, a subaltern with Hojeda, and whose highest naval rank was boatswain's mate, in an expedition that never sailed, managed in this lying world to supplant Columbus, and baptize half the earth with his own dishonest name."

The denunciation is not altogether justified. Vespucci took part in four expeditions (1497, 1499, 1501, and 1503), in which he explored nearly two-thirds of the coastline of South America. In a letter to his patron, Lorenzo de Medici, written in 1502, he said that he had "arrived at a new land which we observed to be a continent." Based on this communication the geographer Martin Waldseemüller suggested in 1507 that the new continent be called "America, because Americus discovered it." The name caught on. Columbus was there first, but he had failed to recognize the enormous significance of what he had discovered.

The issue of the naming of America has never been settled to the satisfaction of all scholars. New claims and theories arise spontaneously, as witness this report in *The Times*, London, on June 20, 1958:

> Sir Wilfred Morton, chairman of the board of Customs and Excise, advances an ingenious theory that America is not after all named after the Italian explorer Amerigo Vespucci, but after an obscure customs collector by the name of A'merrick.
>
> Dismissing the Amerigo theory unlikely anyway — " it would probably have been Vespuccia if they wanted to name it after him" — Sir Wilfred disclosed at a City lunch yesterday that A'merrick was the customs collector at Bristol when Cabot made his epic voyage, and was in fact the man who made the payments to finance the trip. He would certainly have been much in Cabot's mind by the time the latter reached Newfoundland.

The voyages of Columbus and the beginnings of Spanish exploration in the New World alarmed the Portuguese. In 1493 Spain requested Pope Alexander VI to settle the rivalry. A papal Bull of Demarcation assigned to Spain all the land west of a line from the Arctic Pole to the Antarctic at a point "a hundred leagues toward the west and south of the Azores and Cape Verde Islands." Portugal was to have all lands discovered east of this line. In 1494 the line was extended farther westward by a treaty between the two powers. England and France as might be expected paid no attention to this agreement which excluded their claims.

During the half century after the first voyage of Columbus, Spanish navigators, explorers, and *conquistadores* set out in enthusiastic expeditions to the New World to stake their claims. Attracted originally by the possibility of acquiring supplies of commodities in the Far East, the Spaniards shifted their field of vision when reports reached them of fabulous wealth in the New World. It was a vast movement of discovery, conquest, and colonization.

The building of the Spanish empire was a story of conquest in the grand manner, colored by avarice and bigotry. The exploits of Spanish explorers inflamed the imaginations of others, who flocked to the New World. Missionaries accompanied the soldiers and settlers to convert the natives to Christianity. The *conquistadores* became rich beyond their dreams. These men on horseback struck down the prosperous Aztec and Inca civilizations, which now lay prostrate at their feet. They received *encomiendas* — the right to extract service and tribute, in return for which they agreed to civilize the native tribes. In effect, this meant the transplanting of European feudalism and labor system to the new continents. In her Golden Century, Spain profited by Columbus's voyages to acquire a huge empire.

All this was the outcome of the glorious achievement of a man whose discovery was unintentional. Many legends surround the name of the great Admiral, among them the story that he had to convince doubting scholars that the earth was round. In reality, he differed with his critics only on the width of the ocean.

As always the detractors had their word, but a new era had begun in history. A great turning point was reached when those three little ships sailed westward to meet the terrors of an unknown ocean.

A curious wanderlust pursued the Great Navigator even after his death. After his funeral, his body was brought to a monastery in Seville. Then his bones were exhumed and brought over the Atlantic to the cathedral at Santo Domingo, and then to Havana. After the Spanish-American war, the body was finally returned to Seville.

LUTHER BEFORE THE DIET OF WORMS, 1521

"I have done: God help me! Amen!"

IN the early days of Christianity there arose a difference between Arius and Athanasius on interpretation of the Trinity — Father, Son, and Holy Ghost. The key issue was whether or not the Holy Ghost proceeded *from* Father to Son, or *through* Father to Son, hinging on one Greek syllable. The Trinitarian formula, projected originally by Athanasius at the Council of Nicaea in 325 A.D., made all three parts of the Trinity co-equal and co-substantial, but the mystery of dispensation — how One became Three — "is still guarded." Followers of Arius, all those who refused to accept the orthodox creed, were declared to be heretics.

From that point on there was unceasing warfare in Christianity between orthodox and radical. Uncounted numbers of humans lost their lives in struggles between factions — all of whom were supposed to follow Christ's teaching of peace on earth to men of good will. The differences came to a head in the early sixteenth century with the Protestant Revolt and Catholic Counter-Reformation, when Christianity split into two parts. It was another major turning point not only in the history of religion but also in the course of civilization.

The central figure in the drama was Martin Luther (1483-1546), the man who was responsible for a climactic moment in world history. This was the human, dyspeptic, stubborn monk who went to Worms to express his dissent and who returned to Wittenberg a living legend. P. Albert Duhamel described his place in history: "To the rulers of both the Holy Empire and the Holy Church, he had become a growing frustration. They dared not silence him by force and yet they could not allow him to continue unsuppressed; to the rising middle class he had come to symbolize the promise of freedom, to the landless nobility, the possibility of a profitable reorganization, and to the landless peasants, the hope of enfranchise-ment."

Few individuals have influenced their age as much as Luther, and there are few who have aroused such contradictory estimates of character. His defenders say that he was a God-inspired teacher, a man of amiability and goodness. They accept the judgement of Luther given by Phillip Melancthon, a close associate, in his funeral oration: "His heart was true and without falseness, his utterance friendly and kindly." He was "a man of rare intellectual acumen who hated intrigue and cunning," and he was "worthy to stand beside Isaiah, Paul, and Augustine."

To this the critics of Luther reply that he was a man of violent contradictions, unstable, emotional, and neurotic. He suffered from "delirious hallucinations" (Funck-Brentano), "religious melancholia" (A. Hausrath), "a mania for greatness" (A. Harnack), or "a neuropathic disorder" (J. Maritain).

The truth lies somewhere in the middle of these extreme views. Luther was neither God nor devil. He was, indeed, a man of remarkable energy and courage, motivated by deep piety, and possessing great talents. He was bitter in denunciation of his enemies, hard and rough in his writings. He was capable of arousing loyalty in his friends and hatred among his enemies. With his violent temper, he never hesitated to attack what he believed to be wrong and anti-Christian. He gave a clue to his character when he described himself as "boisterous, stormy and altogether warlike, born to fight innumerable monsters, to remove stumps and stones, to cut down thistles and thorns, and to clear the wild woods."

In 1508 the twenty-five-year-old Martin Luther, then an Augustinian friar, was called to the University of Wittenberg, which had been recently established by Frederick the Wise of Saxony. Luther's career as a teacher of philosophy was interrupted toward the end of 1510 by a journey to Rome, where he was shocked by the abuses he observed. Nevertheless, he returned to his university a pious Catholic, with no other thought than to campaign for reform, as many others had done before him. A train of events started which forced him into action and threw upon him the leadership of the whole reform movement that had existed for centuries. Although appointed to the office of district vicar and placed in charge of eleven monasteries of his order, he began to have serious doubts about many practices of the Church, particularly in the matter of indulgences.

According to Catholic doctrine, a priest, acting as the instrument of God, had the right to forgive a contrite sinner who had confessed before him. Such absolu-tion freed the sinner from guilt, but did not absolve him from the penalties which God, or his representative, the priest, imposed. It was, therefore, necessary for the sinner to obtain an indulgence, remitting him from the temporal punishment awaiting him in purgatory. Possessing an indulgence, which might be full (plenary) or partial, the sinner could avoid or mitigate his punishment.

Because the need of the public was great, the granting of indulgences assumed enormous proportions. The income of the Church was large. In 1515 Pope Leo X ordered the granting of indulgences, professedly to raise funds for the rebuilding of

St. Peter's. Albrecht of Brandenburg, Archbishop of Mayence, was to get half the proceeds to pay his debts to the Fugger banking house. Johann Tetzel, a Dominican monk, was entrusted with the task of dispensing indulgences in Albrecht's territory. In his eagerness to obtain as much money as possible, Tetzel sold the indulgences carelessly, on occasion without first insisting upon the penitence of the buyer.

Shocked by the activities of this "ignorant and impudent friar," Luther, according to academic custom, posted his famous Ninety-Five Theses on the doors of the Palace Church at Wittenberg on October 31, 1517. The effect was electric. Within a fortnight, the news was disseminated throughout the Germanies, kindling the popular imagination into heated controversy. It became clear that this was no ordinary monkish quarrel, but that, on the contrary, the first great move in the rupture of the Church had taken place.

During the next few years, Luther was led step by step, against his original intention, to a repudiation of the system in which he had been educated. In 1520 he published three popular pamphlets to state his case before the country. The first, titled *An Address to the Christian Nobility of the German Nation,* called upon the princes of the Germanies to unite and destroy the power of the papacy. Sometimes called the political and social manifesto of the Lutheran Reformation, this treatise was, in effect, a declaration of independence from the papacy. In incisive prose, Luther expressed the convictions and prejudices of the German people. He urged the princes to break down three walls of defense against reform set up by the "Romanists": first, the proposition that the temporal authority had no control over the spiritual; second, that no one except the Pope might interpret the Scriptures; and third, that only the Pope might call a Church council. Then followed a series of proposals for reform.

Luther's second pamphlet, *On the Babylonian Captivity of the Church of God,* subjected the entire system of the Seven Sacraments to attack. He rejected all the sacraments except two, baptism and the Lord's Supper, though he granted that penance might have some value.

The third tract, *On Christian Liberty,* was devoted to a simple exposition of the proposition that every man is his own priest. A Christian, in Luther's eyes, was a free lord over all things, and subject to no man. The soul, he said, needs only the Holy Gospel, the Word of God preached by Christ. Faith alone, without works, makes righteousness and through faith all believers are priests.

Though many details were added later to the Lutheran system, the broad outlines were expounded in these three treatises. Pope Leo X was at first disposed to treat Luther's defection lightly, but he soon realized that the pen of the German heretic was shaking the Church to its very foundations. On June 15, 1520, he sent Johann Maier of Eck to the Germanies with a papal bull of excommunication, in which Luther was called upon to recant or face the wrath of the highest power in Christendom. On December 10, 1520, Luther, surrounded by his students and colleagues, ceremoniously committed the papal bull to the flames with the words: "As thou [the Pope] hast troubled the Holy One of the Lord, may the eternal fire trouble and consume thee!" This act marked a categorical break with the Church, which now faced the most powerful rebellion in its history.

In 1521 the young Holy Roman Emperor-elect, Charles V, who might have been able to check Luther in the beginning of his revolt, was too preoccupied with the affairs of his vast realm to halt the fast-developing crisis. He summoned Luther to give an account of his position before the Diet of Worms. Charles, together with the various princes through whose territory the Wittenberg monk would pass, gave Luther a letter of safe-conduct.

It was almost a triumphal procession. By this time Luther was a national hero who enjoyed widespread support. Here is Luther's own account of his journey to Worms: [1]

> The herald summoned me on the Tuesday in Holy Week, and brought me safe-conducts from the Emperor, and from several princes. On the very next day, Wednesday, these safe-conducts were, in effect, violated at Worms, where they condemned and burned my writings. News of this reached me when I was at Worms. In fact, the condemnation had already been published in every town, so that the herald himself asked me whether I still intended to go to Worms. Though, in truth I was physically afraid and trembling, I replied to him: "I will repair thither, though I should find there as many devils as there are tiles on the house tops." When I arrived at Oppenheim, near Worms, Master Bucer came to see me, and tried to discourage me from entering the city. He told me that Glapion, the Emperor's confessor, had been to see him, and had begged him to warn me not to go to Worms, for, if I did, I should be burned.

After arrival at Worms, Luther appeared before the brilliant assembly of the Emperor, princes, nobles, and dignitaries of the German Church. He declared in plain words that he was the author of the heretical books put on display. "Luther at Worms," wrote Lord Acton, "is the most important and pregnant fact in our history, for there he defied all authority, Pope, council, and Emperor alike." The angry monk spoke to the august Diet: [2]

> Since Your Imperial Majesty and Your Highnesses insist upon a simple reply, I shall give you one — brief and simple but deprived neither of teeth nor horns. Unless I am convicted of error by the testimony of Scripture (for I place no faith in the mere authority of the Pope, or of councils, which have often erred, and which have often contradicted one another, recognizing, as I do, no other guide but the Bible, the Word of God), I cannot and will not retract, for we must never act contrary to our conscience.
>
> Such is my profession of faith. Expect none other from me. I have done: God help me! Amen!

---

[1] M. Michelet, *The Life of Luther Written by Himself*, trans. W. Hazlitt (London, 1898), pp. 79—80.

[2] *Ibid.*, p. 89.

Charles listened in mounting dismay. He professed himself appalled by Luther's "stiff-necked reply," and informed the Diet that he would stake upon his imperial cause all his dominions, his friends, his body and blood, and his life and soul: [3]

> My predecessors, the most Christian Emperors of the German race, the Austrian archdukes, and dukes of Burgundy, were truest sons of the Catholic Church until they died, defending and extending their belief to the glory of God, the propagation of the faith, and the salvation of their souls. Behind them they have left the holy Catholic rites so that I should live and die in them. Until now I have lived with the help of God as a Christian Emperor. It is my privilege to maintain what my forefathers established at Constance and other councils.
>
> A single monk, led astray by private judgment, has set himself against the faith held by all Christians for more than a thousand years. He believes that all Christians up to now have erred. Therefore, I have resolved to stake upon this cause all my dominions, my friends, my body and blood, my life and soul.
>
> We are sprung from the holy German nation and appointed by peculiar privilege to be defenders of the faith. It would be disgraceful as well as an eternal stain upon us and our posterity, if in this day and age not only heresy but also the very suspicion of it were to result from our neglect.
>
> After Luther's stiff-necked reply in my presence yesterday, I am now sorry that I have so long delayed moving against him and his false doctrines. I have made up my mind never again, under any circumstances, to listen to him. Under protection of his safe-conduct he shall be escorted to his home. But he is forbidden to preach and to seduce men with his evil beliefs and incite them to rebellion. I warn you to give witness to your beliefs as good Christians and in consonance with your vows.

Accordingly, Charles induced the Diet to issue the Edict of Worms (1521), pronouncing the ban of the Empire against Luther on the ground that the monk of Wittenberg had disturbed the celebration of the sacraments, scorned the papacy, despised authority, and stirred up the people to dip their hands into the blood of the clergy. Luther was now outlawed by both Church and State.

On his way home from the Diet, Luther was kidnapped by a friendly band of followers, and taken to the Wartburg, a castle near Eisenach. For ten months in solitude he hunted, prayed, composed hymns, engaged in nightly wrestling matches with the devil, issued pamphlets, and set down principles for his followers. His most important work was a translation of the Bible into the German vernacular, intended as a means of bringing the word of God directly to the people. Luther's Bible, based on Greek and Hebrew texts, is a landmark in the history of the German language.

During Luther's seclusion at the Wartburg, some of the more radical of his followers, notable Bodenstein of Carlstadt, threatened to turn the movement into a chaotic revolution. Luther returned to Wittenberg in 1522 and preached several

---

[3] E. Armstrong, *The Emperor Charles V* (London, 1902), I, 70.

sermons in favor of moderation, order, and authority. Meanwhile, he remained under the ban. In 1525 he married Katherine von Bora, an ex-nun, who had deserted her convent after reading Luther's treatises. The marriage between the excommunicated monk and the former nun was denounced by loyal Catholics. Luther, on his part, defended his marriage as the proper solution to the problems created by the tradition of clerical celibacy.

Having rejected the organization of the Catholic Church, Luther now found it necessary to create a new ecclesiastical system. Though the Lutheran Church retained some of the old Catholic doctrines and practices, it made departures in ritual. The program issued on New Year's Day 1525 by the newly nominated Bishop of Pomerania called for only two sacraments (baptism and the eucharist), the abolition of pilgrimages, the elimination of the orders, and permission for the marriage of the clergy. Worship was organized along more popular lines; for example, services were to be conducted in German instead of in Latin. Except in questions of doctrine, control of the new church was given to the governments of the German states and towns.

The humanists at first supported Luther's demands for ecclesiastical reform, but later were repelled by his violent attacks upon Catholicism. The formation of a new church dissipated whatever was left of humanist sympathy. Erasmus, especially, found many of Luther's exhortations excellent, but felt them to be vitiated by his "intolerable faults." "May I be lost," he announced, "if in all of Luther's works there is a single syllable of mine, or if any calumnious book was ever published by me; on the contrary, I do all I can to deter others from issuing such works." The humanists concluded that "the rude and angry monk" had fashioned a new religion fully as dogmatic as the older one. Those scholars who had once supported Luther deserted him when his cause was successful.

Luther wanted a "conservative" break with Rome, but he was not altogether successful in his plan of moderation. One complicating factor was his change of mind about the peasants. He had won their support in the early days of his movement by denouncing the feudal lords as "rascals, hangmen, rogues, and swindlers," although at the time he had relied on the lords for support. The peasants, ground down by taxes, found in Luther's teaching of "Christian liberty" a justification for general social change. In 1525 they expressed their grievances in the dignified *Twelve Articles,* calling for reform based on Christian charity. The princes paid no attention.

The bitterness engendered by centuries of exploitation broke into open revolt. Beginning in southwestern Germany, the rebellion spread throughout the Germanies among downtrodden town workers as well as peasants. Roving mobs destroyed castles and monasteries, and threatened to kill all the "godless" priests and nobles. Alarmed by these events, Luther advised the nobles to kill the rebels "without mercy, like mad dogs." This piece of advice was seized upon by the nobles, who put down the revolt with ferocious savagery. As a result, the peasants sank once more into hopeless misery. The war against the peasants robbed the

Lutheran movement of much of its impetus. Instead of conquering all the German states, the new faith was confined eventually to the northern section of the country.

The Diet of Speyer (1526) decided upon compromise in the matter of Catholics versus Lutherans: each of the German states was at liberty to order its religious affairs as it saw fit. The Diet of Speyer (1529), composed of a compact Catholic majority and a weak Lutheran minority, altered the tolerant decree of the earlier Diet, restored the Catholic worship everywhere, and placed Lutherans under the ban. Thereupon the Lutheran members issued a remonstrance: "We hereby protest that we know not how to, cannot, and may not, concur therein, but hold your resolution null and not binding." The action of this minority group, consisting of six princes and the representatives of fourteen free imperial cities, gave to the party the name of "Protestant," later applied to all those who had withdrawn from the Catholic Church.

For the Diet of Augsburg in 1530, Philip Melanchthon drafted the Augsburg Confession, the most important Protestant statement of belief drawn up during the Reformation and the official creed of the Lutheran churches. Presented in Latin and German to Emperor Charles V, who was determined to reconcile the two faiths, the document was conciliatory in tone. It maintained that its signatories were still faithful to the "ancient Catholic Church." The first part attempted to prove that there was nothing in Lutheran doctrines which was at variance with those of the universal Church "so far as that Church is known in the writings of the Fathers." The second part condemned "abuses in the Church," such as monastic vows, celibacy, compulsory confession, festivals, and fasts. The Pope would not be reconciled, the Confession stated, "and Luther refuses." Charles V, dissatisfied with the document, ordered the Protestants to return immediately to the old Church.

When Charles threatened force, Lutheran princes and burghers joined together in 1531 in the Schmalkaldic League, "Solely for the sake of our defense and deliverance." At this time Charles was concerned that Sultan Suleiman the Magnificent, with a large Turkish army, might march on Vienna for the second time. Busy with this and other equally pressing affairs, he agreed to a truce with the German princes. In the meantime, the Schmalkaldic League was gradually enlarged to the position of a great European power.

Luther died in 1546, but his passing seems to have had but little effect on the subsequent course of the Reformation in the Germanies. Shortly afterward, Charles V declared war on the Protestants, and defeated them in several battles. In the long run, however, his efforts to drive Lutheranism from the Germanies were unsuccessful, and he abandoned the task.

The war was terminated in 1555 by the Religious Peace of Augsburg, which was a compromise. Its main provisions were: (1) Lutheranism was recognized as a separate and independent creed. (2) Each prince was to choose for himself between Catholicism and Protestantism, *cuius regio, eius religio.* No provision was made for any other sect: "All such as do not belong to the two above-mentioned religions shall not be included in the present peace but totally excluded from it." (3) Church property seized by the Lutherans before 1552 was to be retained by them. (4) If an ecclesiastical prince should become a Lutheran, he was to resign and surrender his territories.

By this compromise Protestantism was legalized for about half the population of the Germanies, a proportion maintained thereafter without much alteration. Charles V side-stepped the humiliating task of signing peace by abdicating. He died in 1558 in the cell of a Spanish monastery, complaining in his last days that he had made a serious error by not burning Luther at Worms in 1521. Thus ended the story of the Reformation in the Germanies.

As a new and dynamic religious faith, Lutheranism showed itself to be contagious. Outside the Germanies its strongest foothold was gained in Denmark, Norway and Sweden, as well as among the German populations of Hungary, Transylvania, the German towns along the Baltic, and in Poland. It had many followers in Bohemia, but proportionately fewer in France and England, where it was overshadowed by other movements.

The German religious development was only a part of the entire Reformation movement. Henry VIII's split with the Church on the national issue in England, and the work of Zwingli and Calvin in Switzerland, also played important roles in the story of the Reformation. The international Catholic Church centered at Rome was challenged successfully by national Protestant countries.

Few observers would deny the importance of this great turning point in history. By advocating German control of the German Church, Luther won the support of the new nationalist movement. Millions followed his lead. Christendom was divided. Despite the breakdown into many sects, Protestantism became a powerful influence in human affairs.

THE SPANISH ARMADA, 1588

"God of battles, was there ever a battle
like this in the world before?"

THE COUNTRIES

SINCE the days of Roman glory there had been no such empire in the world. Spain in 1588 boasted of an enormous amount of territory — under her control were Naples and Sicily, the duchy of Milan, and Franche-Comté. In Africa she possessed Tunis, Oran, Cape Verde, and the Canary Islands. In Asia she held the Philippines, the Sunda Islands, and a part of the Moluccas. Across the Atlantic she extended her tentacles into Peru and Mexico, New Spain, Hispaniola, and Cuba, as well as into many other American islands.

This was a glorious spectacle of empire, but the scene was clouded — the tiny Netherlands had revolted against Spain's authority. Belgium was brought back into Spanish control — only Holland and several other states held out. To compensate for the loss of the Netherlands, Spain acquired Portugal and all the fruits of Portuguese maritime enterprise. Truly this was a colossal power.

Pitted against this mighty empire was feeble little England, weak in territory but strong in courage and ambition. The England of 1588 had no Indian or colonial empire. She had made settlements in the New World, but they were as yet undeveloped. Scotland was a separate kingdom, and Ireland was in the throes of revolt. England had lost the last of her possessions in France. And she could not boast of a single foreign power as an ally, with the exception of the Dutch, who were embroiled in their own troubles with Spain.

It was David against Goliath, a small island-state against a mighty world empire, a cocky little midget against a giant.

THE ANTAGONISTS

Philip II (1527–1598) came to the throne in 1556 while Spain was still at the height of her glory. More of a Spaniard than his father, he inherited – in addition to Spain – the Netherlands, Naples, and Spanish America. He tried to assert absolute authority in a country broken up by separatism, and he would tolerate no disobedience. A fervent Catholic, he made it one of the more important goals of his life to extirpate Protestantism in Spain and her possessions. To achieve this end he gave a free hand to the Inquisition, which recommended that heretics be burned to death in a ceremony called *auto-da-fé* ("act of faith").

Saint or sinner? On the one side Philip II was described by his contemporary, Luis Carrera de Cordoba, as a prince of many virtues, a just monarch, a devoted father, and a pious Christian. "He was strong in adversity, restrained in prosperity." To a portion of his subjects he was Philip the Prudent, a saintly symbol of the Catholic Counter Reformation.

On the other side, John Lothrop Motley, the American historian, depicted Philip II as the incarnation of evil, a royal criminal, a murderously cruel fanatic, and an administrator of perfect despotism. To this stern Protestant-moralist view others added the labels of "Devil of the South," "The Spider King," and "Escorial Father of Lies." It is a peculiarity of the historian's craft that two sets of eyes can dwell on the same individual and come up with precisely opposite value judgments.

To nineteenth-century German historian Leopold von Ranke, Philip II was neither saint nor sinner, but simply a human being, a sincere patriot, a defender of the faith. Whatever he was, good Christian or bigot, Philip II was bent on smashing the proud English.

Against this personification of Spanish pride and *dignidad* was pitted the shrewdness of an English queen of extraordinary character and personality. Elizabeth I (1533–1603), daughter of Henry VIII and Anne Boleyn, spent her early years in obscurity. Well educated, she became increasingly vain as she grew older. Ascending the throne at the age twenty-five, she worked hard and governed with rigid economy. Constantly in danger of either overthrow or assassination, she lived to give England one of the most brilliant eras of its history.

"More than a man, and sometimes less than a woman," she never married, and thereby achieved the title of England's Virgin Queen. Her foreign policy was geared to the twin problems of keeping her throne secure and promoting the greatness of her country. After 1586 she was faced with a head-on collision with Spain. Her struggle with Philip II was to force her into moves which revealed clear-headed thinking as well as diplomatic skill. When war came, she was the indomitable leader, who gave inspiration and confidence to her people.

At the critical moment she spoke electric words: "I know I have the body of a weak and feeble woman, but I have the heart and stomach of a King, and a King of England, too; and think it foul scorn that Parma, or Spain, or any prince of Europe, should dare to invade the borders of my realm."

Enmity between the two countries had been building up to a climax. With great skill Elizabeth pursued the traditional Tudor policy of playing one Continental power against the other, in order to prevent any one from achieving dominance. Although both French and Spanish monarchs supported plans to dethrone Elizabeth, they were too much occupied with affairs at home to interfere successfully in English affairs. The English queen allowed several high-placed suitors to ask her hand in marriage, but always retreated when the issue was pressed.

After the execution of Mary, Queen of Scots, Philip II came to the conclusion that, if he were to save England for Catholicism, and stop English raids on Spanish commerce, he would have to invade the island and conquer it. The rivalry was clear-cut — a proud Spanish monarch versus England's Virgin Queen, Catholicism versus Protestantism, and Spanish versus English expansion. Pope Sixtus V, anathematizing Elizabeth and proclaiming a crusade against her, supported Philip in his design to destroy English power on land and sea.

THE CONTENDING FLEETS

Philip II sent a powerful armada to conquer England. There is a detailed catalog in the first volume of Hakluyt's *Voyages*. The number of ships amounted to 150, "each one being sufficiently provided of furniture and victuals." The mariners numbered more than 8,000 the slaves 2,088, the soldiers 20,000 (besides noblemen and gentleman volunteers). "The foresaid ships were of an huge and incredible capacity and receipt: for the whole fleet was large enough to contain the burden of 60,000 tons."

Hakluyt added fascinating statistics. The 64 galleons were of such "huge bigness" that they resembled great castles. Enormous and well-pitched cables were twined about the masts of the ships, to strengthen them against batteries of shot. Some ships were so large that they contained "chapels, turrets, pulpits, and other commodities of great houses." On board were great stores of mules and horses, and whatever else was necessary for a land army. There were 147,000 pipes of wine, sufficient for a half year's expedition. In addition, there were 12,000 pipes of fresh water, and all other necessary provisions such as candles, lanterns, lamps, sails, hemp, ox-hides, and lead to stop holes made by gun shots. Princes and nobles from diverse countries were aboard this great flotilla.

All this had been collected with incredible toil and skill. Nothing exactly like it had ever been seen in the history of the world.

The seamen of the armada were enthusiastic because this was their crusade to bring England back into the Catholic Church. Their ships bore the names of saints and apostles. The men were forbidden to swear, gamble, or consort with loose women. At the masts floated the imperial banner with the figures of Christ and Mary.

Against the collection of Spanish ships, those of the Royal Navy numbered no more than thirty-six, to which were added merchant ships collected in the ports. Exactly 17,472 seamen came forward to man the English fleet. At length there was a total of 191 ships adding to a tonnage of 31,985. The Dutch, on whom the

English had called for help, sent along about 60 ships-of-war not so much dedicated to rescuing England as for their own defense.

There was a secret weapon — an angered English populace aroused by the boasting threats of the Spaniards. Within a short time the whole realm — every corner — was guarded by armed men on horseback and on foot. No funds were spared in the serious business of providing horse, armor, and powder. Volunteers rushed forward offering their services without pay. As in 1940 in the early days of World War II, this was an England which refused to be beaten.

THE CLASH

The two fleets met in the English Channel near the British coast in late July 1588. In a series of involved naval engagements, extending over several days, the Spaniards suffered a catastrophic defeat. Storms and high seas broke upon the invaders with such fury that thousands perished and their bodies were cast up by the seas on British strands. Historian John R. Green described the scene in this passage: [1]

> The Spanish ships which remained had no sooner reached the Orkneys than the storms of the northern seas broke on them with a fury before which all concert and union disappeared. Fifty reached Corunna, bearing ten thousand men stricken with pestilence and death. Of the rest some were sunk, some dashed to pieces against the Irish cliffs. The wreckers of the Orkneys and the Faroes, the clansmen of the Scottish Isles, the kernes of Donegal and Galway, all had their part in the work of murder and robbery. Eight thousand Spaniards perished between the Giant's Causeway and the Blaskets. On a strand near Sligo an English captain numbered eleven hundred corpses which had been cast up by the sea.

Sir John Hawkins, who took part in the battle, revealed what happened while fighting was still in progress as he wrote:

> My bounden duty humbly remembered unto your good lordship. I have not busied myself to write often to your lordship in this great cause, for that my lord admiral doth continually advertise the manner of all things that doth pass. So do others that do understand the state of all things as well as myself.
>
> We met with this fleet somewhat to the westward of Plymouth upon Sunday in the morning, being the 21st of July, where we had some small fight with them in the afternoon. By the coming aboard of one of the other of the Spaniards, a great ship, a Biscayan, spent her foremast and bowsprit, which was left by the fleet in the sea, and so taken up by Sir Francis Drake the next morning. The same Sunday there was, by a fire chancing by a barrel of powder, a great Biscayan spoiled and abandoned, which my lord took up and sent away. The Tuesday following, athwart of Portland, we had a sharp and long fight with

---

[1] J. R. Green, *A Short History of England* (London, 1916), p. 420.

them, wherein we spent a great part of our powder and shot, so as it was not thought good to deal with them any more till that was relieved.

The Thursday following, by the occasion of the scattering of one of the great ships from the fleet which we hoped to have cut off, there grew a hot fray, wherein some store of powder was spent; and after that little done until we came near to Calais, where the fleet of Spain anchored, and our fleet by them; and because they should not be in peace there, to refresh their water or to have conference with those of Duke of Parma's party, my lord admiral, with firing of ships, determined to remove them; as he did, he put them to the seas; in which broil the chief galleass [2] spoiled her rudder, and so rode ashore near the town of Calais, where she was possessed of our men, but so aground that she could not be brought away.

That morning being Monday, the 29th of July, we followed the Spaniards, and all that day had with them a long and great fight, wherein there was great valor showed generally by our company. In this battle there was spent very much of our powder and shot; and so the wind began to blow westerly, a fresh gale, and the Spaniards put themselves somewhat to the northward, where we follow and keep company with them. . . .

Our ships, God be thanked, have received little hurt, and are of great force to accompany them, and of such advantage that with some continuance at the seas, and sufficiently provided of shot and powder, we shall be able, with God's favor, to weary them out of the sea and confound them. . . .

At their departing from Lisbon the soldiers were twenty thousand, the mariners and others eight thousand; so as in all, they were twenty-eight thousand men. Their commission was to confer with the Prince of Parma, as I learn, and they proceed to the service that should be there concluded; and so the duke to return into Spain with these ships and mariners, the soldiers and their furniture being left behind. Now this fleet is here and very forcible, and must be waited upon with all our force, which is little enough. There should be an infinite quantity of powder and shot provided and continually sent abroad.

And so, praying to God for a happy deliverance from the malicious and dangerous practice of our enemies, I humbly take my leave. From the sea, aboard the Victory, the last of July, 1588.

The Spaniards take their course for Scotland; my lord doth follow them. I doubt not, with God's favor, but we shall impeach their landing. There must be order for victual and money, powder and shot, to be sent after us.

Your lordship's humbly to command,

JOHN HAWKINS

Sir Walter Raleigh, who participated with distinction in the destruction of the Spanish Armada, wrote an account, published in Hakluyt's *Principal Navigations,* immortalizing the last fight of the *Revenge*, a narrative which is the inspiration for

---

[2] A three-masted galley, with guns on each side.

Tennyson's celebrated poetic interpretation: *"God of battles, was ever a battle like this in the world before?"*

Raleigh's story of the *Revenge*:

The rumors are diversely spread, as well in England as in the low countries and elsewhere, of this late encounter between her Majesty's ships and the Armada of Spain; and the Spaniards, according to their usual manner, fill the world with their vain-glorious vaunts, making great appearance of victories, when on the contrary themselves are most commonly and shamefully beaten and dishonored, thereby hoping to possess the ignorant multitude by anticipating and forerunning false reports. . . .

And it is no marvel that the Spaniards should seek by false and slanderous pamphlets, advisos, and letters, to cover their own loss, and to derogate from others their due honors (especially in this fight, being performed far off), seeing they were not ashamed in the year 1588, when they purposed the invasion of this land, to publish in sundry languages in print, great victories (in words) which they pleaded to have obtained against this realm, and spread the same in a most false sort over all parts of France, Italy, and elsewhere. . . .

The Spanish fleet, having shrouded their approach by reason of the island, were now so soon at hand as our ships had scarce time to weigh their anchors, but some of them were driven to let slip their cables and set sail. Sir Richard Grenville was the last weighed, to recover the men that were upon the island, which otherwise had been lost. The Lord Thomas with the rest very hardly recovered the wind, which Sir Richard Grenville not being able to do, was persuaded by the master and others to cut his mainsail and cast about, and to trust to the sailing of his ship; for the squadron of Seville were in his weather bow. But Sir Richard utterly refused to turn from the enemy, alleging that he would rather choose to die, than to dishonor himself, his country, and her Majesty's ship; persuading his company that he would pass through the two squadrons in despite of them, and enforce those of Seville to give him way. Which he performed upon divers of the foremost, who, as the mariners term it, sprang their luff, and fell under the lee of the Revenge. But the other course had been the better, and might right well have been answered in so great an impossibility of prevailing. Notwithstanding out of the greatness of his mind he could not be persuaded.

In the meanwhile, as he attended those which were nearest him, the great San Philip, being in the wind of him, and coming toward him, becalmed his sails in such sort as the ship could neither way nor feel the helm: so huge and high cargoed was the Spanish ship, being of a thousand and five hundred tons; who after laid the *Revenge* aboard. When he was thus bereft of his sails, the ships that were under his lee, luffing up, also laid him aboard; of which the next was the admiral of the Biscayans, a very mighty and puissant ship commanded by Brittan Dona. The said Philip carried three tiers of ordnance on a side, and eleven pieces in every tier. She shot eight forthright out of her chase, besides those of her stern ports.

After the *Revenge* was entangled with this Philip, four others boarded her, two on her larboard, and two on her starboard. The fight thus beginning at three of the clock in the afternoon continued very terribly all that evening. But the great San Philip, having received the lower tier of the *Revenge*, discharged with crossbar shot, shifted herself with all diligence from her sides, utterly misliking her first entertainment. Some say that the ship foundered, but we cannot report it for truth, unless we were assured.

After the fight had thus without intermission continued while the day lasted and some hours of the night, many of our men were slain and hurt, and one of the great galleons of the Armada and the Admiral of the Hulks both sunk, and in many other of the Spanish ships great slaughter was made. Some write that Sir Richard was very dangerously hurt almost in the beginning of the fight, and lay speechless for a time ere he recovered. . . .

All the powder of the *Revenge* to the last barrel was now spent, all her pikes broken, forty of her best men slain, and most part of the rest hurt. In the beginning of the fight she had but one hundred free from sickness, and four score and ten sick, laid in hold upon the ballast. A small troop to man such a ship, and a weak garrison to resist so mighty an army! By those hundred all was sustained, the volleys, boardings, and enterings of fifteen ships of war, besides those which beat her at large. On the contrary the Spanish were always supplied with soldiers brought from every squadron, all manner of arms, and powder at will. Unto ours there remained no comfort at all, no hope, no supply either of ships, men, or weapons; the masts all beaten overboard, all her tackle cut assunder, her upper work altogether razed; and, in effect, evened she was with the water, but the very foundation or bottom of a ship, nothing being left overboard either for flight or defense.

Sir Richard finding himself in this distress, and unable any longer to make resistance, — having endured in this fifteen hours' fight the assault of fifteen several armadas, all by turns aboard him, and by estimation eight hundred shot of great artillery, besides many assaults and entries, and that himself and the ship must needs be possessed by the enemy, who were now cast in a ring round about him, the *Revenge* not able to move one way or other but as she was moved by the waves and billow of the sea, — commanded the master gunner, whom he knew to be a most resolute man, to split and sink the ship, that thereby nothing might remain of glory or victory to the Spaniards, seeing in so many hours' fight, and with so great a navy, they were not able to take her, having had fifteen hours' time, fifteen thousand men, and fifty and three sail of men-of-war to perform it withal; and persuaded the company, or as many as he could induce, to yield themselves unto God, and to the mercy of none else, but, as they had, like valiant resolute men, repulsed so many enemies, they should not now shorten the honor of their nation by prolonging their own lives for a few hours or a few days.

The master gunner readily condescended, and diverse others. But the Captain and the Master were of another opinion and besought Sir Richard to have care of them, alleging that the Spaniard would be as ready to entertain a composition as they were willing to offer the same, and that there being divers sufficient and valiant men yet living, and whose wounds were not mortal, they might do their country and prince acceptable service hereafter.

A few days after the fight was ended, and the English prisoners dispersed into the Spanish and Indian ships, there arose so great a storm from the west and northwest that all the fleet was dispersed, as well the Indian fleet which were then come unto them, as the rest of the Armada which attended their arrival. Of which, fourteen sail, together with the *Revenge* (and in her two hundred Spaniards), were cast away upon the isle of St. Michaels. So it pleased them to honor the burial of that renowned ship the *Revenge*, not suffering her to perish alone, for the great honor she achieved in her lifetime.

AFTERMATH

The legend of Spanish invincibility was shattered as a result of this crushing defeat. England no longer feared invasion. Thereafter, English sea dogs turned on Spanish commerce with even greater zest, and succeeded almost completely in driving Spanish shipping from the seas. Although they had to renew their fighting spasmodically throughout the duration of Elizabeth's reign, the English retained their mastery of the seas.

This turning point was the supreme disaster of Philip's reign. From the English point of view, it was the most decisive battle since Hastings, serving England and delivering a heavy blow to Spanish prestige. The entire world could see now that the Spanish monster was a giant with feet of clay. The country which had seized the limits of the then known world had overextended itself. With the Armada was destroyed an illusion, and Spain slid downward into decadence. England assumed the mantle that had slipped from the Spaniards. This was the beginning of the history of the great British Empire.

ROUT OF THE TURKS AT VIENNA, 1683

"Let us through to kiss the hands of valor."

THERE is an intriguing story of how nineteenth-century Chinese war lords fought their battles. The rivals would meet in a tent and go through an elaborate tea ceremony, each leader dropping hints as to the number of men he had available, the size and firepower of his weapons, and his prospects for victory. Then the two would balance accounts, with one admitting that, because his enemy was stronger and deserved the victory, he, himself, would accept the role of loser and pay reparations. The conflict thus settled, the two armies went their separate ways without loss of life. All-important face was saved.

Unfortunately, this highly intelligent method of waging warfare was an exception to the rule of brutal force in human affairs. The great clincher in contact between tribes, peoples, and nations nearly always has been naked power – the dominance of might, the settling of issues by battle. By far the majority of turning points in history fit into this category of power struggle.

Many confrontations fit into a religious pattern, including the major conflicts between Crescent and Cross. We have seen how Islam was stopped in its tracks at Tours in 732 A.D., when it tried to sweep into Western Europe in a wide arc through Spain. That was discouraging, but the Muslims did not consider it a final defeat. There would be another attempt to assault Western Christendom, this time from the east and under Turkish auspices. The outcome was still another great turning point in history.

In the seventh century A.D. the Ottoman Turks, who had merged with other tribes of Turanian stock, were converted to the Islamic faith. Their imperial power was centered in Asia, but they looked always to expansion in Europe. Because the

Seljuk branch could not maintain its empire against assaults by the Crusaders, its place was taken by the stronger tribe of Ottomans. The latter managed to overrun all the territory in Asia that had been within the boundaries of the Roman Empire. They even made some headway into Europe.

Pope Pius V encouraged the organization of an allied force (Austria, Venice, Genoa, Sicily, Naples, and Spain) in fear of the growing Turkish power in the Mediterranean. On October 7, 1571, a naval battle was fought at Lepanto in the Gulf of Corinth between a Turkish fleet of 273 galleys under Ali Pasha and an allied European fleet of about 200 galleys commanded by Don John of Austria. The result was a crushing blow to Muslim sea power.

In the late seventeenth century the Turks tried again, this time seeking a decision on land. Taking advantage of internal disputes in Austria, Kara Mustafa Pasha, Turkish grand vizier, led a huge army toward Vienna in 1683. Terrified, the Austrian emperor and his court fled from the capital, leaving the city defended by only 10,000 troops of its regular garrison under Count von Stahremberg, who stubbornly refused to surrender. The small army was soon in desperate straits. The Turks were on the verge of victory when the Austrian cause was suddenly bolstered from the outside in support which was as unexpected as it was welcome. John Sobieski, King of Poland, accompanied by several German princes and their armies, marched to the relief of the Christian city. Attacking the Turks from the rear, Sobieski's force inflicted a disastrous defeat upon them.

Sobieski's rescue has been termed "the last noble reflex of the great crusading impulse of the Middle Ages." Certainly it was a unique service rendered by one people to another in an age of Machiavellian diplomacy and national selfishness. The rout at Vienna, a terrific blow to the Turks, was the beginning of their expulsion from Eastern Europe. By the end of the century they were forced to yield rich slices of the Balkans to Poland, Austria, and Venice.

In the following letter, dated September 13, 1683, hero Sobieski gave his wife an eyewitness account of his rescue of Vienna.

The Lord be praised forevermore for granting our nation such a triumph and such glory unrivalled in history! The entire camp of the enemy, with all their artillery and great treasures, has fallen into our hands. They are now retreating in great confusion. The approaches to the town, the camp, and the fields are covered with their corpses.

The camels and other beasts of burden, the cattle, and the sheep of the enemy were captured to-day by our soldiers and the captive Turkish shepherds driven off.

Some deserters, beautifully appareled and well-mounted, have voluntarily come over to us. So extraordinary was their appearance that the townspeople were overcome with fright. Our soldiers were astonished, for they believed that the enemy had recovered and were coming back for further battle.

The losses of the enemy in powder and ammunition alone is worth a million. Several of our camp followers very foolishly set off the powder in several places, making a fearful noise, but no further damage was done. The grand vizier lost all his rich treasure and just managed to escape, on horseback, with nothing but the coat on his back.

It happened this way. Having forced my way into the enemy's camp, I hurried forward in pursuit of the vizier when one of his chamberlains surrendered to me. He afterwards showed me the tent of his leader. This tent was so large that it might have contained within its circumference the city of Warsaw or Lemberg. The standard which the grand vizier always had carried before him with great ceremony fell into my hands, as did the Muslim banner given to him by the sultan for his campaign. The latter I sent by post to his Apostolic Holiness in Rome. Our army now possesses quantities of the most gorgeous goldmounted sabers and other rare Turkish equipment.

The coming of night prevented us from continuing our pursuit. It cannot be denied that the enemy defended himself bravely, especially the company of foot-guards who guarded the approaches to the camp and bore the brunt of the battle. A part of these daring and courageous Janizaries fought with us in the field, while the rest sought to storm the fortifications.

I estimate the number of the besieging army at three hundred thousand, not counting the Tartars. Others say there were three hundred thousand tents with three men to a tent, but that would make the number altogether too great to be believed. Yet, there must have been at least one hundred thousand tents. From each of these the victors take what they like. Even the townspeople are rushing out to take their share of the booty. I guess that it will take at least eight days to gather in all the spoils.

Some of the Austrian people — especially women — who had been taken captive by the Turkish army and who could not be taken away in flight, were cut down by saber. Many of them, however, can be healed of their wounds.

Early this morning I went into the town and learned that it could not have held out five days longer. Never have the eyes of men looked on such great damage done in so short a time. The enemy's mines smashed great masses of stone and rock and tossed them about in heaps. The imperial castle is riddled by holes and ruined by Turkish cannon balls.

The vizier threw his entire force against my right wing, so that my troops of the left wing had little to do, and finally left their position and came to my aid.

When the victory was won, I was surrounded by Prince Von Waldeck, the elector of Bavaria, and many of the imperial princes, who embraced and kissed me. The generals clasped my hands and feet. The other commanders, with their regiments on horse and on foot, shouted: "Our brave king!"

Early this morning came the Elector of Saxony and the dukes of Lorraine, who could not speak to me yesterday because their position was on the outermost edge of the left wing. Finally, Count von Stahremberg, the governor of Vienna, accompanied by a huge crowd of people of all social classes, came to greet me, kissing and embracing me and calling me their savior.

Later I visited two churches, where once more I found mobs of people who sought to kiss my hands, and even my feet and clothing. Most of them had to be content with touching my coat. One could hear them crying everywhere: "Let us through to kiss the hand of valor!" All shouted for joy. I begged the German officers to forbid this, but in spite of them a great crowd shouted loud: "Long live the King!"

There is a huge pile of captured tents and flags. The enemy has departed with nothing but his life. Let Christendom rejoice and thank the Lord our God that he has not permitted the heathen to scorn and ridicule us with such words as: "Where, now, is your God?"

King John hit the Oriental invaders hard, and saved the city, a triumph not only for him but for Western civilization. Vienna was safe and the Turks were retreating. The outcome was another major alliance against the Turks — Austria, Venice, Poland, Russia, Malta, Tuscany, even the papacy. All joined in a new crusade, but they made only minor gains.

The battle of Vienna recapitulated the battle of Tours — in both cases a Christian society made a successful stand against Muslim invaders. In each battle there was a chance that Western Christendom might succumb to Islam, but Christian power was finally triumphant.

NEWTON'S *PRINCIPIA* REVOLUTIONIZES THE SCIENTIFIC WORLD, 1687

"If I have seen farther than Descartes,
it is by standing on the shoulders of giants."

HISTORICAL turning points are not limited to the political and religious spheres. The story of man's sojourn on this planet includes not only his physical but also his intellectual development. The human imagination is an awesome thing, and to it may be attributed many if not most of the discoveries and inventions by which men have conquered their environment. In this framework the contribution of Newton is of crucial importance and one that marks another great change in human affairs.

Behind the Newtonian synthesis was a story of compounding enlightenment. The cultural character of Western European society during the first two centuries of the modern era took shape in the esthetic revolt of the Renaissance and the religious revolt of the Reformation. Both the Renaissance and the Reformation were conterminous with European economic expansion, the rise of the middle class, and the development of national states. Each expressed in different ways a reaction against the all-embracing authority of the medieval Church, but significantly, both Renaissance and Reformation ended in a sort of compromise with medieval philosophy. The Renaissance humanists were intellectually immature – though dissatisfied with the medieval emphasis upon Aristotelian "science," they made no attempts to discover rational solutions for the problems of mankind. Similarly, the leaders of the Reformation, though at odds with Catholic authority, founded their national churches in the same sort of authoritarianism that had characterized the medieval Church. Both Renaissance and Reformation had modern aspirations, but medieval vestiges. Some historians feel that they were closer to the Middle Ages than to modern times.

In contrast the eighteenth-century Era of Enlightenment (or Age of Reason) resulted from a rational movement. Since the time of the Hellenistic Greeks, Western Europe had forgotten or avoided the methods of scientific discovery. During the sixteenth century, a few hardy souls attempted to take up the broken threads of science, but their voices were lost in the noise of theological disputes and humanistic quarrels.

The rationalist movement already under way in the seventeenth century burst forth in full glory in the late eighteenth century. Our modern culture is a direct outgrowth of this intellectual revolution. This was a new Age of Faith — faith in the rational behavior of nature and in immutable natural laws, and also belief in man's ability to discover these laws and to perfect his life and his world.

The decay of medieval orthodoxy left the scholars of Western Europe perplexed. Humanism failed to provide an acceptable substitute for the medieval teleological explanation of phenomena and events. Scholars eventually began to search for new ways of eliciting the secrets of the universe, and for some infallible method of solving man's problems. They found the key in natural laws governing the universe and society.

The first contributions to modern science were in astronomy. Throughout the Middle Ages, the geocentric theory of Claudius Ptolemy, a celebrated Alexandrian mathematician and astronomer who lived in Egypt in the second century A.D., was accepted as indisputable. According to Ptolemy, the earth was an immovable sphere, fixed in the center of the universe, while the sun and stars moved around it. The Ptolemaic system harmonized well with appearances. Did not the sun rise in the east and set in the west?

In the middle of the sixteenth century a new theory of celestial mechanics replaced the old Ptolemaic system. According to this revolutionary theory, the universe is heliocentric (sun-centered). Outstanding among the supporters of the heliocentric theory was the Polish astronomer Nicholas Copernicus (1473–1543). In 1530 Copernicus virtually completed his *De Revolutionibus Orbium Coelestium (Concerning the Revolution of the Heavenly Bodies);* it was published in 1543 and remade the science of astronomy on an inverted design. Copernicus suggested that the sun remains stationary, while the planets, including the earth, circulate around it. This startling proposition encountered opposition from the theologians, for in denying that the earth is the center of the universe it contradicted the doctrine that the earth and the universe were created to serve the needs of man.

Copernicus cagily dedicated his book to Pope Paul III, but nevertheless, it was condemned as subversive, and later was placed in the Index. The prohibition continued from 1616 to 1757. Catholic and Protestant theologians alike condemned the Copernican theory as foolish, absurd, and opposed to Scripture. For many centuries the Ptolemaic system had been accepted because it seemed to harmonize with Christian doctrines; now it was demonstrated scientifically to be false. To scholars the implications were astonishing.

In spite of the unfavorable circumstances surrounding its appearance, the new theory gradually won acceptance. The Copernican revolution swept man from his position as the central figure in the universe, making him "a tiny speck on a third-rate planet revolving about a tenth-rate sun drifting in an endless cosmic ocean."

An Italian philosopher, Giordano Bruno (c. 1548–1600), following the lead of Copernicus, made another attack on the Ptolemaic system. Bruno came to these conclusions: (1) there is neither a center nor a limit to the universe, because everything is relative to the point of observation; (2) there are a number of universes besides our own; (3) there are no fixed starry spheres, because the heavenly bodies move freely in space. These brilliant intuitions were subsequently confirmed.

Bruno regarded himself a pious Christian, but he aroused the wrath of the Church. His hypothesis concerning the plurality of worlds and universes contradicted the account of Creation in Genesis, and was a serious challenge to the principles of Christianity. Churchmen were particulary disturbed because Bruno explained his theories in popular language, thus stimulating "heretical thoughts." He was excommunicated, and burned at the stake in 1600.

Tycho Brahe (1546–1601), a Danish astronomer, was not altogether convinced of the validity of the Copernican theory, yet he contributed to its final acceptance. He built a remarkable astronomical observatory called the "Castle of Heaven" on an island between Denmark and Sweden. He devised a number of instruments far better than those used by his predecessors. Though he added little to astronomical theory, he compiled a large amount of data which was used to good advantage by later scientists. In perfecting the art of pre-telescopic observation, in locating scores of fixed stars, and in preparing the most valuable stellar charts of his day, Tycho Brahe stimulated other scholars in the work of discovering the new universe.

The wealth of data accumulated by Tycho Brahe was utilized by his brilliant German assistant, Johann Kepler (1571–1630). Kepler, a scientist of unlimited imagination, turned from observation and record-keeping to theory. He became the founder of modern physical astronomy. During his early career, though a convinced Copernican, he accepted the traditional belief that all celestial revolutions must be performed in fixed circles; but after years of calculations, he came to the conclusion that the planets traveled freely in space around elliptical orbits. His epoch-making "third law of planetary motion," [1] which appeared in 1619 in his *De Harmonice Mundi (The Harmonies of the World)*, described a system of celestial movements depending on the varying velocities of the planets. By perfecting a geometrical plan of the solar system, Kepler enhanced the powers of astronomers to predict future phenomena. This work helped to shatter the old Ptolemaic and Aristotelian conceptions of planetary motion.

The next important figure in the astronomical revolution was Galileo Galilei

---

[1] Kepler's third law states that the squares of the periods of circulation round the sun of the several planets are in the same ratio as the cubes of their mean distances. The sun is the "solitary auditor" of the celestial system.

(1564–1642), an Italian mathematician and physicist. Though at first disposed to accept the traditional cosmology as satisfactory, Galileo was persuaded, after reading Kepler, to join the ranks of the Copernicans. With his improved telescope, Galileo ascertained that the spots on the moon were valleys and not the "stains of Adam's sins," that the Milky Way was a great collection of stars, and that the moon owed its light to reflection from the sun. He discovered four satellites of Jupiter, which he found were not stationary but actually revolved around the planet. In addition, he detected sunspots, from which he inferred the rotation of the sun. These observations convinced him of the fundamental truth of Copernican theories.

Galileo also made important contributions to dynamic mechanics. In 1581, when only seventeen, he observed a lamp swinging in the cathedral of Pisa, and discovered the law of the pendulum: whatever the range of the oscillations, they were always executed in the same interval of time. In 1589, at the age of twenty-five, he demonstrated to the naked eye that bodies of differing weights fall with the same velocities. He also proved that the path of a projectile is a parabola. These and other discoveries aroused the hostility of ecclesiastical authorities, who found them at odds with passages in the Scriptures. Summoned before the Inquisition at Rome in 1633, Galileo was forced to recant, and, as penance, was enjoined to recite the seven penitential psalms once a week for three years.

The ablest of the early telescopic observers, Galileo made his discoveries easily intelligible to the general public. Unfortunately, both Galileo and Kepler ignored each other's work in the field of planetary motion. Had they worked together, it is possible that Galileo's practical dynamic mechanics and Kepler's generalizations might have resulted in an earlier discovery of the universal force of gravitation. As it was, both scholars paved the way for Newton.

The revolution in celestial mechanics was accompanied by a revolution in mathematics and physics. A French philosopher, René Descartes (1596–1650), laid the groundwork for that exactness in observation and calculation which was to become the basis of modern science. Descartes was a pioneer in mathematics, the founder of analytical geometry — the application of algebra to geometry. His system of notation, classification of curves, geometric interpretation of negative quantities, and contributions to the theory of equations have survived to the present day.

The language of mathematics, conceived by Descartes, enabled scientists to express their conclusions more accurately and clearly. His work was vital for scientists because it enabled them to prove that nature is an integral whole, operating according to mathematical laws. This approach conflicted with the Aristotelian conception, accepted throughout the Middle Ages, that nature consists of a variety of unrelated objects, each of which attempts to fulfill its aim in its own way. In studying the laws of nature, the rationalists relied heavily upon mathematics, rather than theology. Nothing, it was now said, is accidental or arbitrary in nature; everything is ruled by universal mathematical laws.

All this intellectual activity led straight to the crowning achievement of seventeenth-century science — Newton's law of gravitation. Here was a giant stride forward not only in physical science but in the cultural history of the Western world. According to the French mathematician Legrange, Newton was "the greatest genius that ever existed and the most fortunate, for we cannot find more than once a system of the world to establish." "The law of gravitation," wrote William Whewell, "is indisputably and incomparably the greatest scientific discovery ever made, whether we look at the advance which it involved, the extent of the truth disclosed, or the fundamental nature of this truth." Lord Macaulay stated: "In no other mind have the demonstrative faculty and the inductive faculty co-existed in such supreme excellence and perfect harmony."

Newton's genius flowered early. He was born on December 25, 1642, the posthumous son of a yeoman farmer. It was said that as a young lad he showed little interest in books until a successful fight with another youngster aroused in him a spirit of emulation and the desire to become head boy at his school. He made his first experiment as a young man of sixteen when a great storm raged over England. To find out the force of the wind, he first jumped with and then against it, and by comparing these distances with the extent of his jumps on a calm day, he was able to compute the force of the storm. With the financial assistance of an uncle, he matriculated in 1661 at Trinity College, Cambridge, on a poor man's scholarship. He remained at Cambridge for more than thirty years, first as student, then as fellow, and from 1669 on as successor to his teacher, Isaac Barrow, in the chair of mathematics. Newton's name has been linked since then with Cambridge and Trinity College.

Newton's discoveries in optics, the invention of differential calculus, and the law of gravitation were made before he was twenty-five. For the first time he worked out the binomial theorem. He began his scientific work in optics and color in 1665. That same year, according to Voltaire, the fall of an apple in a garden started him on a train of thought leading to the discovery of universal gravitation.

It was not until 1687 that Newton published his immortal *Philosophiae Naturalis Principia Mathematica*. With this work he consolidated and brought to a climax the earlier contributions of Copernicus, Kepler, and Galileo. The foundation for building an exact interpretation of physical phenomena was completed. Now there was a general set of principles for physical science.

Recognizing the validity of Galileo's law of falling bodies and Kepler's laws of planetary motion, Newton synthesized and combined them in his own law of universal gravitation. The planets revolve around the sun in harmony with Galileo's law of falling bodies. From one of Kepler's laws, namely, the proportionality of the areas to the time of their description, Newton inferred that the force that retained the planet in its orbit was always directed to the sun. From another one of Kepler's laws, namely, that every planet in our universe describes an ellipse around the sun, Newton drew the more general inference that the force by which the planet moves around the focus varies inversely as the square of the distance therefrom. He demonstrated that a planet acted upon by such a force could not move in any other curve than a conic section. Moreover, this force of attracting existed even in the smallest particle of matter. From all this Newton outlined the universal law of gravitation — *"Every particle of matter is attracted by or gravitates to every other particle of matter with a force inversely proportional to the squares of their distances."*

Newton's identification of terrestrial gravitation with the mutual attraction of the planets was the result of accurate mathematical comparisons. His great contribution was demonstrating the mechanical consequences of gravitation throughout the whole solar system. He showed gravitation to be the basic factor governing the movements of the planets. He explained the figure of the rotating earth by its action on the minuter particles of matter. He demonstrated how the tides and the precision of the equinoxes worked on the same principle. Finally, he accounted for some of the more striking lunar and planetary inequalities.

Newton's account in his *Principia* of how he arrived at the law of gravitation gives an indication of the rationalist's mind at work. In the past, he said, scholars had sought to explain the phenomena of the heavens and the seas by the power of gravity, but they had not yet been able to assign the cause of this power. Certainly, it must proceed from a cause that penetrates to the very center of the sun and planets, without suffering the least diminution of its force. It operates not according to the quantity of the surfaces of the particles upon which it acts (as mechanical causes used to do), but according to the quantity of the solid matter that they contain. It extends to immense distances, decreasing always in the duplicate proportions of the distances. Gravitation toward the sun is made up out of the gravitations toward the several particles of which the body of the sun is composed. In receding from the sun, gravitation decreases accurately in the duplicate proportion of the distances as far as Saturn.

Hitherto, Newton confessed, he had not been able to discover the cause of those properties of gravity from phenomena:

> I frame no hypothesis; for whatever is not deduced from the phenomena is to be called an hypothesis; and hypotheses, whether metaphysical or physical, whether of occult qualities or mechanical, have no place in experimental philosophy. In this philosophy particular propositions are inferred from the phenomena, and afterwards rendered general by induction. Thus it was that the impenetrability, the mobility, and the impulsive force of bodies, and the laws of motion and gravitation were discovered. And to us it is enough that gravity does really exist, and act according to the laws which we have explained, and abundantly serves to account for all the motions of the celestial bodies, and of our sea.

Newton's law of gravitation marked the closing of an epoch in the history of human thought and the beginning of a new era. The nature of the cosmos as propounded by Aristotle, Ptolemy, and the medieval astrologers was overthrown and placed in the category of outmoded knowledge. In its place appeared a new cosmic theory of infinite scope and complexity. The earth was demoted from its pre-eminent plane and became only one tiny, relatively unimportant planet in a maze of planets. The sun became just one star in a system of thousands of millions of stars. The entire system became one galaxy in a universe of thousands of millions of galaxies. Man was permanently removed from his proud position at the center of creation and was unceremoniously shoved into an inferior place. He was now regarded as an infinitesimal organism, a physical machine composed of atoms and molecules, and governed by natural laws. But, as compensation, he was rescued from a universe of chance and superstition and given one of unfailing orderliness.

This — the orderliness of the universe — was the supreme discovery of science in the Age of Reason. Painstaking observations and calculations had proved that celestial phenomena occur at regular sequences, often complex, but always systematic and invariable. The running of no clock ever approaches in precision the motions of the heavenly bodies. To this day, clocks are corrected and regulated by comparing them with the apparent motions of the planets.

Newton's achievement was the construction of a world-machine: instead of a series of planets, each going its own way independent of all others, the universe now appeared as a well-ordered, mechanical whole, held together by gravity. This revelation of the power of the scientific method led almost immediately to its application to other fields, including social and political problems. From this time on, science became a cultural force of the utmost importance — a true intellectual revolution.

The instigator of this turning point in history remained unaffected by the extravagant praise accorded him. Newton's reaction was an exercise in modesty: "I was like a boy playing on the seashore, and diverting myself in now and then finding a smoother pebble and a prettier shell than ordinary, whilst the great ocean of truth lay undiscovered before me."

FALL OF THE BASTILLE, 1789

*"Though ye dream of lemonade and epaulettes,
ye foolish women!"*

"THE FRENCH Revolution," wrote Leo Gershoy, "was the dramatic acceleration of tendencies and developments which had their roots in the past. Material events and systematic speculations prepared it.... Under the pressure of two simultaneous sets of circumstances, those of resistance and civil war within and opposition from without, for both of which the revolutionists were partly to blame, the course of the development grew swifter and deeper. It cut its way into the profound layers of national life and into the hidden and savage recesses of the human spirit." [1]

It is incorrect to assume that the French Revolution was a sudden isolated event, or to describe it only in dramatic pictures of barricades on the streets of Paris and the execution of aristocrats on the guillotine. Nor can it be ascribed to the irresponsible mischief of the eighteenth-century philosophers. To maintain that the French Revolution just happened, or was caused by the evil machinations of one king, class, or historical factor, is to mistake the very meaning of history. Revolutions are not produced by magic — they are rather the products of a combination of forces, circumstances, and leaders. And often they become major turning points in history.

For centuries before 1789 the way of life of European men had been changing. Thoughts, desires, traditions, and customs were transformed. Then, with apparent suddenness and with great violence, the upheaval occurred. Old institutions were shattered by the powerful new forces of modern times. The principles of the old

---

[1] Leo Gershoy, *The French Revolution* (New York, 1932), p. 4.

social order – the *Ancien Régime* – with its autocratic monarch and its privileged nobility, were repudiated. The Revolution became a watershed – a point of departure for the history of modern times.

To all corners of Europe the ideas that shaped the history of the nineteenth and twentieth centuries were diffused from Paris. Modern nationalism emerged out of revolutionary France. The concept of democracy found a most potent expression in principles underlying the French Revolution. Likewise, liberalism, with its accent on orderly, constitutional development, had its roots in revolutionary France. In a very real sense the French Revolution was the dynamic materialization of a new concept of liberty which conflicted with the old principle of obedience to authority and tradition.

The desire for political liberty was strongest among the Parisian bourgeoisie, who, having obtained economic power, were determined to win political dominance and to legalize gains already made. The middle class had the most to gain by overthrowing the existing antiquated social order.

Eighteenth-century society in France, as that in most of Europe, was composed of privileged and unprivileged orders. The government was autocratic, commerce was restricted. Such conditions persisted at a time when the people could no longer tolerate them. The French *philosophes* flayed the Old Regime and fashioned the theoretical framework of a new order. Accusing the absolute monarch and the aristocracy and clergy of maintaining the worst abuses of feudalism, the *philosophes* demanded a transformation of society. The culminating point was reached when the middle and lower classes combined to overthrow the privileged orders.

Louis XVI, weak and irresolute, dreading civil war above all else, had to concede the triumph of the Third Estate, the hitherto unprivileged order. Chagrined when the French Guard refused to fire upon the people in Paris, he ordered the remainder of the nobility and clergy to join in the deliberations of the National Constituent Assembly. By this action he sanctioned the political revolution, although at the same time, under the influence of the queen and her "infernal cabal," he dismissed finance minister Necker, and appealed for aid to Swiss and German mercenaries.

Meanwhile, the situation in Paris became critical. The news of Necker's dismissal dismayed the moneyed bourgeoisie, who feared that a reactionary finance minister might lead the country into bankruptcy. A new and more disturbing element now appeared – the Parisian mob, composed of hungry workingmen, the unemployed, city vagrants, and criminals, all demanding food. The king, uncertain of support by the French Guard, relied upon foreign troops. The bourgeoisie organized a civil militia to protect life and property against foreign troops as well as against Frenchmen. Angered citizens, motivated by hunger and the flaming speeches of demagogues, broke into the food stores and bakeries and pillaged the gunshops.

To obtain more arms to defend the Assembly, the mob, on July 14, 1789, proceeded to the Bastille, a prison and the chief arsenal of Paris, thoroughly hated as a symbol of royal despotism. Within a short time, the revolutionists, bolstered by the French Guard, forced the surrender of the garrison, massacred the commander and several of the Swiss guards, freed the small number of prisoners, and razed the ancient prison. The expected counterattack by foreign mercenaries did not materialize. Thomas Carlyle described it in his flamboyant style: [2]

> In the Court, all is mystery, not without whisperings of terror; though ye dream of lemonade and epaulettes, ye foolish women! His Majesty, kept in happy ignorance, perhaps dreams of double-barrels and the Woods of Meudon. Late at night, the Duke de Liancourt, having official right of entrance, gains access to the Royal Apartments; unfolds with earnest clearness, in his constitutional way, the Job's news. *"Mais,"* said poor Louis, *"c'est une revolte."* ("Why, that is a revolt!") "Sire," answered Liancourt, "it is not a revolt – it is a revolution."

Thomas Jefferson, drafter of the American Declaration of Independence at the age of thirty-three, looked forward to years of peaceful living. But his wish was not fulfilled, for his country had first call upon his services. From his arrival in Paris in 1784 until his departure in the fall of 1789, he served as a special envoy and as American minister to France. "It is you, sir, who replace Dr. Franklin?" Frenchmen would ask him. "No one can replace him, sir. I am only his successor," Jefferson would tactfully reply. Present himself at the mass demonstration against the use of foreign troops, Jefferson was staying at this time at the home of Monsieur de Corny, spokesman for the people in presenting their demands to the governor of the Bastille. From de Corny he heard firsthand an account of the storming of that notorious prison which triggered the revolution.

> The King was now (July 11, 1789) in the hands of men, the principal among whom had been noted, through their lives, for the Turkish despotism of their characters, and who were associated around the King, as proper instruments for what was to be executed.
> The news of this change (of ministry as well as the plan to use foreign troops to crush the revolution) began to be known at Paris about one or two o'clock. In the afternoon a body of about one hundred German cavalry were advanced and drawn up in the Place Louis XV, and about two hundred Swiss posted at a little distance in their rear. This drew people to the spot who thus accidentally found themselves in front of the troops, merely at first as spectators, but as their number increased their indignation rose. They retired a few steps and posted themselves on and behind large piles of stones, large and small, collected in that place for a bridge was to be built adjacent to it.
> In this position, happening to be in my carriage on a visit, I passed through the lane they had formed without interruption. But the moment after I had passed the people attacked the cavalry with stones. They charged but the advantageous position of the people and the showers of stones obliged the horse to retire and quit the field altogether, leaving one of their number on the

---

[2] Thomas Carlyle, *The French Revolution* (London 1891), Part I, Book V. p. 156.

ground, and the Swiss in the rear not moving to their aid. This was the signal for universal insurrection, and this body of cavaliers to avoid being massacred, retired toward Versailles.

The people now armed themselves with such weapons as they could find in armorer's shops and private houses and with bludgeons; and were roaming all night, through all parts of the city, without any decided object. The next day, the Assembly pressed on the King to send away the troops, to permit the Bourgeoisie of Paris to arm for the preservation of order in the city, and offered to send a deputation from their body to tranquillize them; but their propositions were refused. A committee of magistrates and electors of the city were appointed by those bodies, to take upon them its government. The people, now openly joined by the French guards, forced the prison of St. Lazare, released all the prisoners, and took a great store of corn, which they carried to the corn-market. Here they got some arms, and the French guards began to form and train them.

The city committee determined to raise forty-eight thousand Bourgeoisie, or rather to restrain their numbers to forty-eight thousand. On the 14th they sent one of their members (Monsieur de Corny) to the Hôtel des Invalides, to ask arms for their Garde Bourgeoise. He was followed by, and he found there, a great collection of people. The Governor of the Invalides came out and represented the impossibility of his delivering arms without the orders of those from whom he received them. De Corny advised the people then to retire, and retired himself; but the people took possessions of the arms. It was remarkable that not only the Invalides themselves made no opposition, but that a body of five thousand foreign troops, within four hundred yards, never stirred.

M. de Corny and five others were then sent to ask arms of M. de Launay, Governor of the Bastille. They found a great collection of people already before the place, and they immediately planted a flag of truce, which was answered by a like flag hoisted on the parapet. The deputation prevailed on the people to fall back a little, advanced themselves to make their demand of the Governor, and in that instant a discharge from the Bastille killed four persons of those nearest to the deputies. The deputies retired. I happened to be at the house of M. de Corny when he returned to it, and received from him a narrative of these transactions.

On the retirement of the deputies the people rushed forward, and almost in an instant were in possession of the fortification of infinite strength, defended by one hundred men, which in other times had stood several regular sieges and had never been taken. How they forced their entrance has never been explained. They took all the arms, discharged the prisoners and such of the garrison as were not killed in the first moment of fury, carried the Governor and Lieutenant Governor to the Place de Grève (the place of public execution), cut off their heads and sent them through the city, in triumph, to the Palais Royal. About the same instant, a treacherous correspondence having been discovered in M. de Flesselles, Prevôt des Marchands, they seized him in the Hôtel de Ville and cut off his head.

These events, carried imperfectly to Versailles, were the subject of two successive deputations from the Assembly to the King, to both of which he gave dry and hard answers; for nobody had as yet been permitted to inform him, truly and fully, of what had passed at Paris. But at night, the Duke de Liancourt forced his way into the King's bedchamber, and obliged him to hear a full and animated detail of the disasters of the day in Paris. He went to bed fearfully impressed.

The decapitation of de Launay worked powerfully through the night on the whole Aristocratic party, insomuch that in the morning those of the greatest influence on the Count d'Artois represented to him the absolute necessity that the King should give up everything to the Assembly. This according with the dispositions of the King, he went about eleven o'clock, accompanied only by his brothers, to the Assembly, and there read them a speech in which he asked their interpositions to re-establish order.

The demolition of the Bastille was now ordered and begun. A body of the Swiss guards, of the regiment of Ventimille, and the city horse guards, joined the people. The alarm at Versailles increased. The foreign troops were ordered off instantly. Every Minister resigned.

The King came to Paris, leaving the Queen in consternation for his return. Omitting the less important figures of the procession, the King's carriage was in the center; on each side of it, the Assembly, in two ranks a foot; at their head the Marquis de La Fayette, as Commander-in-chief, on horseback, and Bourgeois guards before and behind. About sixty thousand citizens, of all forms and conditions, armed with the conquests of the Bastille and Invalides, as far as they would go, the rest with pistols, swords, pikes, pruning hooks, scythes, etc., lined all the streets through which the procession passed, and with the crowds of people in the streets, doors, and windows, saluted them everywhere with the cries of *"vive la nation,"* but not a single *"vive le Roi"* was heard.

The King stopped at the Hôtel de Ville. There M. Bailly presented, and put into his hat, the popular cockade, and addressed him. The King being unprepared, and unable to answer, Bailly went to him, gathered from him some scraps of sentences, and made out an answer, which he delivered to the audience, as from the King. On their return, the popular cries were *"vive le Roi et la nation."* He was conducted by a Garde Bourgeoise to his palace at Versailles, and thus concluded an *"amende honorable,"* as no sovereign ever made, and no people ever received.

In this manner the excited mob killed the governor of the Bastille and freed the seven prisoners found in its cells. Later it became clear that attackers were looking for ammunition for firearms. But a much stronger motivation was the desire to capture the old fortress as a symbol of that despotism which had put political offenders under lock and key without any attention to due process of law. Curiously, not one of the seven inmates of the Bastille released on that fateful day was a political prisoner, but that was merely a strange circumstance in an emotion-loaded expedition.

When the king ordered foreign troops to take over the city, he was urged by the representatives of the National Assembly to withdraw them. He refused, whereupon the outraged citizens decided to defend the Assembly. It was a motley army, rather than an uncontrolled mob, which stormed the fortress-prison. The Third Estate now had fighting men to help assure the success of the Revolution.

The mobs of Paris captured the Bastille, but it now remained for the townsmen and villagers to level the bastilles of feudalism. Peasants throughout the provinces burned down the châteaux of their lords, plundered the castles, and tried to destroy the records of manorial dues. Some of the the more far-sighted noblemen left their lands and sought refuge elsewhere. Those who insisted upon maintaining their privileges were left to face pitchforks and scythes. The feudal idea of property rights, already weakened by abuses, was swept away.

Thus, in this highly dramatic fashion, began the great revolution of early modern times and one of the more significant turning points in the history of civilization. Without knowing it the men who set fire to the battered old prison turned the mainstream of history in a new direction.

It is an understatement to say that vital changes came after the fall of the Bastille. The French Revolution meant a decline in the fortunes of the old privileged classes as well as the coming of age of the bourgeoisie. It marked the triumph of the secular state after long centuries of ecclesiastical control, and it legalized the separation of Church and State. It stimulated the appearance of modern nationalism, certainly the most potent sociopolitical force of our times. The sentiment of nationalism emerging out of the French Revolution became, in the words of Norman Angell, "more important than civilization, humanity, decency, kindness, pity; more important than life itself." And even today, in an age when communications have made the world much smaller and people speak of international cooperation, nationalism persists as quarreling states refuse to relinquish even a small part of their sovereignty.

The mythical Scarlet Pimpernel was credited with performing deeds of valor in rescuing aristocrats from the tumbrils and prisons during the Terror in Paris. But not even that fictional giant was able to turn back the tide of change. In the pain of revolution a new world was being born.

NAPOLEON'S RETREAT FROM MOSCOW, 1812

"My campaign is only beginning."

INDISPUTABLY a great man, or vicious dictator? For generations historians have been fascinated by the personality and career of this little Corsican, who emerged from obscurity to take control of France and become the most powerful man in the world. To some he is a source of inspiration, a superman who brought honor, glory, and prestige to France, while to others he is a vile, bloodthirsty creature, a barbarian midget ensconced in the seat of the mighty.

Certainly he was one of the great military geniuses of history. For him war was the highest of arts, and few human beings understood its complexities as well as he. An advocate of a carefully planned defense, he led his enemies to give battle under the most unfavorable circumstances, confused them with rapid action, and then destroyed them. He left nothing to chance: the size and quality of the opposing forces, the weather, the psychology of the enemy as well as that of his own troops, the range of weapons, the terrain, the availability of alternative positions, supplies, and a hundred other factors. He supervised even the most insignificant of details in his campaigns. His attention to every phase of strategy was in itself a weakness, for with the increasing size of armies it became difficult for him to guide a huge military machine without making costly errors. Yet, most of his campaigns were models of brilliant strategy.

Napoleon remained loyal to his family, evidence of the clannishness characteristic of his background. Although he was Corsican in personality, he was at the same time influenced by his French environment. His overwhelming ambition was due to a combination of factors — the poverty of his youth, the responsibility of helping to provide for his family, and his unprepossessing appearance. He permitted nothing to stand in the way of his aspirations — not his love for Josephine, nor the life of a Bourbon pretender to the throne, nor the lives of thousands of Frenchmen. Selfish, egotistic, cynical, unscrupulous, he had a blind faith in his star of destiny. A man of prodigious energy, he could work for twenty hours at a stretch and then regain his strength in a few hours of sleep. Eliminating all who dared defy him, he bestrode the world like a colossus until he himself was struck down.

By 1810 Napoleon was lord of a domain stretching from Paris to Rome and Hamburg, and comprising one hundred and thirty departments. Included were France, the eastern half of the Italian peninsula (to a point south of Rome), Belgium, Holland, and German territory to the Rhine and eastward to Hamburg. The Confederation of the Rhine, the Grand Duchy of Warsaw, the Kingdom of Italy, the Kingdom of Naples, Switzerland, and the Kingdom of Spain were under French control. Denmark and Norway, Prussia, and Austria were in alliance with Napoleon, and dependent upon him. Only Great Britain, Russia, Turkey, Sweden, Portugal, Sardinia, and Sicily remained free.

The "Little Corporal" had nearly won the goal of a United States of Europe under his own leadership.

The bitterness engendered throughout Europe against the conqueror appeared in Robert Southey's *Ode,* written in that very year, 1810. The poet called for justice against "that accursed head":

> Who counsels peace at this momentous hour,
> When God hath given deliverance to the oppress'd,
>   And to the injured power?
> Who counsels peace, when Vengeance like a flood
> Rolls on, no longer now to be repress'd
>   When innocent blood
> From the four corners of the world cries out
>   For justice upon one accursed head;
> When freedom hath her holy banners spread
>   Over all nations, now in one just cause
>   United; when with one sublime accord
>   Europe throws off the yoke abhorr'd,
> And Loyalty and Faith and Ancient Laws
>   Follow the avenging sword?

Notwithstanding its outer magnificence, the Napoleonic empire began to disintegrate rapidly. Military genius was not enough to seal the cracks in an edifice built on a weak foundation. Napoleon had made himself lord of Continental Europe, but he had not been able to subjugate one enemy. As long as England survived, she could be expected to stir up rebellion among the conquered nations. There was also danger from a regenerated Prussia, which had recovered from her crushing defeat in

1806. Napoleon lost the support of Catholics in 1809, when he accused Pope Pius VII of admitting English goods to papal territory; he ended the argument by incorporating the Papal States into the French empire, and then took the venerable pontiff to Fontainebleau as a prisoner. Napoleon's alliances, particularly the Russian, were insecure. Even members of his family and favorites he had raised to positions of power proved to be disloyal.

Napoleon's alliance with Russia was shaken by a growing estrangement. Clearly there had to be an eventual end to conquest, but Napoleon, slave of his own ambitions, was unable to stop. Alexander I, who had once promised to uphold Napoleon's Continental System, [1] found that it had reacted to Russia's disadvantage, and refused to enforce it any longer. Moreover, the Russian czar had been alienated at Tilsit in 1807 by Napoleon's refusal to permit him to take Constantinople. Still another grievance in Moscow was Napoleon's marriage to Marie Louise of Austria, a step which made it impossible for Russia to "rectify" her frontiers at the expense of Austria.

Napoleon decided to strike at Russia and force her submission. He gathered an enormous army of "twenty nations," composed of his allies and dependencies, and awaited a favorable moment.

He chose June 22, 1812, which turned out to be a most unpropitious day for invaders of Russia. On June 22, 1941, Adolf Hitler shouted to the German people as his armies rolled across the plains of eastern Poland into Russia: "I decided today again to lay the fate and future of the German Reich and our people in the hands of our soldiers." It was also an unwise decision.

On that fateful June 22 Napoleon addressed the *Grande Armée* as he opened his Russian campaign: "Soldiers, the second war of Poland has commenced. Russia offers us the alternative of dishonor or war. The choice does not admit of hesitation. Let us march forward!"

The confident Napoleon believed himself to be well prepared for invasion. At his disposal he had a huge army composed of 500,000 infantry, 100,000 cavalry, and armed with 1,400 field and siege guns. Opposed to him were two Russian armies, one of about 127,000 men commanded by Barclay de Tolly, and the other numbering 43,000, led by Prince Bagration.

Napoleon's plan was simple – to separate the two opposing armies and fall on them with overpowering strength one at a time. It was precisely the same strategy later to be used by Hindenburg, Ludendorff, and Hoffman in August 1914 when they advanced on Russian generals Rennenkampf and Samsonov and defeated them separately. In this case the Germans were helped considerably by the desire of each Russian general to win all the glory himself by smashing his way directly to Berlin without letting the other know exactly where he was. This was dangerously unintelligent procedure in warfare.

---

[1] A blockade of Britain begun by Napoleon in the Berlin Decree of November 21, 1806 and seeking to enforce the closing of Continental ports to British commerce.

On June 24, 1812, Napoleon's *Grande Armée* crossed the Niemen at Kovno and Grodno, forcing Barclay back, Four days later the French captured Vilna and stayed there until July 16. It was a fatal delay, for it allowed the two Russian armies to unite at Smolensk by August 1. Two weeks later Napoleon attacked again, but the wily Russians withdrew in fairly good order. Already the vast French army was suffering from an epidemic of colic and severe sunstroke. Serious straggling began.

Armchair strategists with hindsight hold that Napoleon would have done better had he decided to go into winter quarters at this point and wait until the following spring before venturing farther into the Russian steppes. But it was not as easy as it sounds. The supply problem was always a difficult one, and besides, enemy troops might have fallen on Napoleon's rear. If he abandoned the campaign at this point, it meant a triumph for his enemies, and that he could not tolerate. He decided to push on to Moscow and force the Russians to come to terms.

By this time Barclay was replaced by the flamboyant Marshal Kutusov, and that meant no rest for the invaders. On September 7 there was a bloody encounter at Borodino, the Russians losing 38,000 killed and wounded, and the French 25,000. But Napoleon pushed on to Moscow.

Incompetence and nepotism at and near the top contributed to the rout of the invaders. For six weeks Napoleon lingered amid the charred ruins of Moscow under the delusion that the Russians would sue for peace. "My campaign is only beginning," he declared. Then the retreat began. The invading army disintegrated into a disorderly mob. Insubordination, far more deadly to morale than the pursuing Cossacks or even the notorious Russian winter, was the major factor in the decimation of Napoleon's forces.

At the end of November the retreating French army managed to reach the Beresina River. Bridges were hastily constructed while the Russians closed in for the kill. The crossing continued amid scenes of panic, as thousands drowned or were trampled under foot. Tolstoy described the catastrophe in *War and Peace*: "At the broken-down bridge of Beresina the woes, which had till then come upon them in a sort of regular succession, were suddenly concentrated there in a single moment – in one tragic catastrophe, which remained printed on the memory of all."

The Russian pursuit ended at the Niemen, but the *Grande Armée* had already done so thorough a job of destroying itself that only a small remnant lived to see France again. Tolstoy likened the plight of Napoleon's forces to that of a wounded beast "that feels its death at hand, and knows not what it is doing. Very often the wounded creature, hearing a stir, rushes to meet the hunter's shot, runs forward and back again, and itself hastens its own end."

There are several excellent eyewitness accounts of the crossing of the Beresina. The selection below is adapted from an account by Wairy Louis Constant, Napoleon's valet.

The day before the passage of the Beresina was one of dreadful solemnity. The Emperor seemed to have come to his decision with the cold resolve of a man who attempts a despairing deed; nevertheless, a council was held. It was decided that the army should despoil itself of all useless burdens which might impede its march. Never was there more unity in its opinions; never was deliberation more calm; it was indeed the calm of men who commit themselves for the last time to the will of God and their own courage. The Emperor ordered the eagles of all the corps brought together and they were burned. He thought there was nothing else for fighters to do. It was a sad spectacle, these men stepping from the ranks one by one, and throwing down what they loved more than life itself. I have never seen more profound dejection, nor shame more bitterly felt.

By five o'clock of the evening of November 25th temporary trestles, made of beams from the cabins of the Poles, were fixed above the stream. Not being strong enough, the beams gave way shortly after five. It was now necessary to wait until the next day, and the army once more relapsed into gloomy conjectures. It was plain that it would have to sustain the fire of the enemy the next day, but there was no room for choice.

It was only at the end of that night of anguish and sufferings of every kind that the first trestles were driven down into the river. It is difficult to understand how the men could stand up to their mouths in water full of floating ice, summoning all the strength with which nature endowed them and all the remaining courage born of energy and devotion in order to drive piles several feet deep into the miry river bed; struggling against the most horrible fatigues; pushing away with their hands enormous masses of ice which would have knocked them down and submerged them by their weight; fighting, in a word, and fighting unto death with cold — the greatest enemy of life.

Well, that is what our French pontonniers did. Several of them were either dragged down by the currents or suffocated by the cold. That is a glory, it seems to me, which outweighs many another.

The Emperor awaited daylight in a poor hut. Great tears flowed down his cheeks which were paler than usual. He appeared to be overwhelmed by his grief.

Before the bridge was finished, some four hundred men were partially transported from the other side of the river and two miserable rafts which they could with difficulty steer against the current. From the shore we were able to see them greatly shaken by the huge chunks of ice which clogged the river. These masses would come to the very edges of the raft; meeting an obstacle, they would stop for a while and then be drawn underneath those feeble planks and produce horrible shocks. Our soldiers would stop the largest ones with their bayonets and make them deviate insensibly beyond the rafts.

The impotence of the army was at its highest point. The current forced the poor horses to swim obliquely across, which doubled the length of the passage. Then came the masses of ice which, striking against their chests and sides, inflicted piteous wounds.

When the artillery and baggage wagons were crossing, the bridge was so thronged that it collapsed. Instantly a backward movement began, which thrust together in horrible confusion all the stragglers who were shuffling along, like driven cattle, in the rear of the artillery. Another bridge had been hastily constructed, perhaps with the belief that the first might give way, but the second was narrow and unprotected by railings at the sides. However, at first it seemed to be a very useful makeshift in such an appalling calamity.

But how disasters follow one upon the other! The stragglers rushed to the second bridge in droves. The artillery and baggage wagons, in a word all the army supplies, had been in advance on the first bridge when it broke. By the sudden recoil which took place, the catastrophe became known. Then those behind were the first to gain the other bridge. It was necessary that the artillery should cross first. It rushed impetuously toward the only road to safety which remained.

It would be difficult for any pen to describe the scene of horror which then took place. Conveyances of all kinds reached the bridge only over a road of trampled human bodies. One could see for himself how much brutality and cold-blooded ferocity are produced in human minds by the instinct of self-preservation. There were some stragglers, the craziest of all, who wounded and even killed with bayonet thrusts their unfortunate horses who did not obey the whips of their drivers. Several wagons had to be abandoned in consequence of this odious proceeding.

The bridge, as I have said, had no ledges at the sides. Many of those who forced their way across fell into the river and were sucked down beneath masses of ice. Others sought to save themselves by grasping the miserable planks of the bridge; they remained suspended above the abyss until their hands, crushed by the wheels of the carriages, would lose their hold; then they dropped to rejoin their comrades and were engulfed by the waves. Entire caissons with drivers and horses were catapulted into the water.

Poor women were seen holding their children out of the water, as if to retard their death by a few moments, and the most frightful of deaths. A truly admirable maternal scene . . . of which we have seen the touching reality.

Some officers harnessed themselves to sleds to pull their comrades who were rendered helpless by their wounds. They wrapped the unfortunate ones as warmly as possible, cheered them up from time to time with a glass of brandy when they could get it, and gave them the most touching attention.

On the 29th the Emperor left the banks of the Beresina, and we went to pass the night at Kemen. His Majesty occupied a wretched wooden building. A freezing wind penetrated it from all sides through the windows, nearly every pane of which was broken. We closed the openings as well as we could with hay.

On the 3rd of December we arrived at Malodeczno.

The Emperor left in the night. By daybreak the army had learned the news. The impression it made cannot be described. Discouragement was rampant. Many soldiers cursed the Emperor and reproached him for abandoning them. There was a universal cry of malediction.

On the night of the 6th the cold increased greatly. Its severity may be imagined: birds were found on the ground frozen stiff. Soldiers seated themselves with their heads in their hands and their bodies bent forward in order to relieve the emptiness in their stomachs. Some were found dead in that position. When we breathed, the vapor of our breath congealed in our eyebrows. Tiny white icicles formed in the beards and mustaches of our soldiers; to get rid of them they would warm their chins at the bivouac fires, and as one may fancy, a good many did not do so with impunity. The artillerymen held their hands on the noses of their horses, seeking a little warmth from the powerful breath of their horses.

How disastrous was that retreat!

The Marquis de Chambray added a significant footnote: "At Beresina ended the career of the *Grande Armée*, which had made Europe tremble; it ceased to exist in a military sense, its only safety now lay in headlong flight." Napoleon handed over supreme command to one of his generals, Murat, and together with a few others set out for Paris. Disgusted, he denounced "the Russian colossus," insisting that she was the enemy of all Europe. In much the same way Adolf Hitler was later to excoriate the Russians for not knowing when they were defeated.

On December 18, the humiliated emperor rode through the Arc de Triomphe, and alighted at the central entrance of the Tuileries. In Russia he had left behind his finest troops frozen into stiff corpses. His strategy had been to force the capitulation of the English by achieving mastery of the East. But his plan was frustrated by events in Russia.

The Russian debacle of 1812 produced a wave of fresh enthusiasm among the many peoples still under the Napoleonic yoke. The reaction was especially strong in Prussia, which like most of Europe, longed for freedom from French domination. The retreat from Moscow was a turning point not only in the career of Napoleon but in the whole story of Western civilization. The conqueror eventually sustained a decisive final defeat at Waterloo and ended his days a prisoner of the despised English.

THE COMMUNIST MANIFESTO, 1847–48

"Workingmen of all countries, unite!"

A BEARDED man of nervous temperament sits at a desk in the British Museum. He is bothered by boils on his neck and an uncontrollable urge to revolutionize a decadent society in which he saw no social justice. From an obscure corner of the British library came the impetus for world revolution, a manifesto which sounded a rallying cry for social change.

Few publications have matched the impact of that pamphlet. It became not only the bible of the Communist Party but also the instruction book for global revolution. Today half the population of Europe and a third of the people on earth — totalling more than a billion — live in official Communist societies which owe their way of life to this little pamphlet.

The man with the sharp eye and untidy beard was Karl Marx (1818-1883), the son of a lawyer in the Prussian Rhineland and a journalist by profession. He studied law and philosophy and began a career as political journalist and publicist. At Cologne he founded the *Rheinische Zeitung*, which was soon suppressed. From 1843 to 1845 he lived in Paris, where, after reading Proudhon, he was converted to socialism. Expelled from France, he returned to Germany, from which he fled at the time of the revolution of 1848. He ultimately made London his permanent home, and there, taking advantage of a free environment, he planned his blueprint to overthrow the society he so deplored.

Marx had an intellectual partner who also helped solve some of his more immediate financial problems. Friedrich Engels, the son of a well-to-do textile manufacturer, was also dissatisfied with the society in which he lived. After several years of writing for Chartist journals, he went to Paris, where he met Marx. The two joined the Communist League, also called the League of the Just, and they subsequently worked together in a lifetime relationship.

Both Marx and Engels were well versed in the history of socialism. The idea was by no means new. Plato in his *Republic* projected an ideal society which, though aristocratic, was based on communal ownership:

> In the first place, no one shall possess any private property, if it can possibly be avoided; secondly, no one shall have a dwelling or storehouse into which all who please may not enter; whatever necessaries are required by temperate and courageous men, who are trained to war, they should receive by regular appointment from their fellow citizens, as wages for their services; and they should attend common masses and live together as men in a camp . . . they should be forbidden to handle gold or silver. . . . If they follow these rules, they will be safe themselves and the saviors of the city, but whenever they come to possess lands, and houses, and money of their own, they . . . will become hostile masters of their citizens, rather than their allies; and so they will spend their whole lives, hating and hated, plotting and plotted against.

There was also an element of socialism in Thomas More's *Utopia* (1516), which described society in which there would be a community of goods, work for all, a national system of education, and a milieu in which the welfare of all citizens was placed above that of the individual. The pre-Reformation Albigensians and Lollards preached a kind of Christian socialism which was said to be based on Christ's original teachings, and the Anabaptists set up communist organizations.

The idea of modern socialism was conterminous with the rise of large-scale industry. Reformers, appalled by unsanitary factory conditions as well as the wretched life of the working masses, called for an end to *laissez-faire* capitalism on the ground that it did not let anything, not even human life, stand in the way of profits.

The first movement was called Utopian Socialism, a humanitarian concept which favored socialist colonies. Claude Henri de Saint-Simon favored this precept: "The whole of society ought to strive toward the amelioration of the moral and physical existence of the poorest class; society ought to organize itself in the way best adapted for attaining this end." He recommended a social system in which each man would be placed according to his capacity, and rewarded according to his works.

Another Frenchman, François Fourier, recommended the formation of social units called phalanges, each numbering about 1,600 people, all with common occupations and all sharing in the produce. Robert Owen, an English businessman and philanthropist, also tried to organize cooperative communities along socialist lines. He was certain that, once disorderly competition was eliminated, there could be unlimited prosperity.

Utopian Socialism was not successful in gaining the support of either the capitalists or the workers. Any radical change in the structure of society was unwelcome to capitalists. The workers were confused by an idea which they did not understand. Isolated intellectuals who favored the movement were ridiculed as impractical visionaries.

Both Marx and Engels rejected the solution proposed by the Utopian Socialists. In late 1847 they drew up the *Communist Manifesto* as a kind of platform for an international gathering of workingmen in London. The pamphlet traced the history of the working-class movement, surveyed critically the existing socialist literature, and explained the outlines of communism. Starting with the materialistic interpretation of history and using Mill's labor theory of value, Marx and Engels spoke of an inescapable class struggle, the inevitable triumph of the proletariat, and the establishment of the Communist state.

The *Communist Manifesto* began with these oft-quoted words: "A spectre is haunting Europe – the spectre of Communism," and ended with a battle cry: "Workingmen of all countries, unite!" In between was the core of Communist theory.

Marx later published his *Das Kapital* (1867-1894), a giant work which elaborated the ideas presented in the *Communist Manifesto*. Without going into the fine points, let us consider for a moment the five basic elements in Marxism:

Marx and Engels presented what they called "scientific socialism." There are five main elements in Marxism:

Economic Interpretation of History: Economic forces are basic. All major changes in history are due to changes in the mode of production, and the consequent changes in men's relations to each other. Social, political, religious, and cultural institutions are regarded as a superstructure on the economic foundation. In other words, man's spiritual life is considered to be dependent upon and derivative from his material life.

When the economic structure changes, the superstructure must also change. But as the class structure of society is highly resistant to modification, political and social developments lag behind economic changes. The resultant disharmony, contrary to natural law, forces a drastic readjustment, usually through revolution. Then the old superstructure of society crashes in ruins, and a new one, "more in harmony with economic conditions," comes into existence.

Class Struggle.   According to Marx and Engels, the process by which this readjustment is accomplished is the class struggle. The basis of this theory is an outgrowth of Hegelian dialectic, although Marx "stood Hegel on his head." Hegel conceived of the history of the world as a continuous conflict of ideas: each idea (thesis) has its negation (antithesis), and out of the resulting struggle between them arises a new and higher idea (synthesis), which in turn becomes a new thesis, to do battle in its turn. The history of civilization, in Hegel's estimate, was the story of this conflict of ideas from the time of the oriental despots to that of "the highest form of society – the Prussian monarchy."

Marx accepted the general form of Hegelian dialectic, but for the battle of ideas, he substituted the struggle of economic forces and classes. Thus, one class, elevated to power by economic forces, automatically brings into existence an antagonistic class. With the concentration of power in the hands of the capitalists, the proletariat becomes consolidated, develops a will of its own (opposing that of its master), turns upon its oppressors, and finally overthrows them. Then the workers form a new socio-political superstructure more in consonance with the forces of production.

Theory of Surplus Value.   A third principle of Marxian Socialism, the theory of surplus value, was a main theme of *Das Kapital.* Any commodity produced under capitalistic enterprise is "a mass of congealed labor-time." In other words, the value of any commodity is determined primarily by the amount of socially necessary labor required to manufacture it. In reality, the modern worker produces more than enough to provide for himself a decent standard of living. But the capitalist pays the worker only a subsistence wage (which is the current market price for the labor power consumed), and keeps for himself the far greater share of the proceeds. The residue left after the worker is paid his small pittance was termed surplus value; from it the capitalist draws his interest, rents, and profit. Marx concluded that if the laborer works ten hours a day, and only five hours' labor are needed to pay for his subsistence, he creates surplus value for his employer in the amount of five hours of work.

Internationalism.   Marx affirmed that all the workers of the world are comrades, members of that class which has "the historic mission of bringing about a better social order." Their interests transcend the limits of national loyalties. The national interests of the workers are identical with their international interests. He urged the adoption of a new battle cry: "Workingmen of the world unite; you have nothing to lose but your chains."

Inevitability.   This development, said Marx, is inevitable. It is useless in the long run to attempt to prevent the creation of a new society which is already developing in the body of the old. Either the new class, representing the new economic forces, triumphs or society itself crashes in ruins after fratricidal strife. The rationalists of the late eighteenth century had applied the idea of natural law to nature, religion, government, and society; Marx went one step farther by applying it to history. History thus becomes a science; the broad trends of the future can be predicted. In this view, the approaching revolution which Marx predicts will be final, emancipating the last class in history, and creating a classless society. Man's primitive period will end, and he "will make the final leap from the realm of necessity into the realm of freedom."

This bare framework of teaching has been interpreted in varying ways by followers of Marx — all the way from the democratic socialism of Rosa Luxemburg to the ironfisted dictatorship of Joseph Stalin. Just as the seemingly simple teachings of Christ have been variedly interpreted by dozens of sects each claiming exclusive truth, so have the ideas of Marx been disseminated in differing colors when seen through the prism of political expediency.

Anti-Marxist critics attack all five principles of Marxism as faulty. They declare that the economic interpretation of history is exaggerated, for political, social, cultural, and religious factors are often more than mere "ideological veils" for the fundamental economic factors. Moreover, they say, the concept of materialism fails to take into consideration the spiritual elements in human nature.

Critics of Marxism further contend that the idea of the class struggle falls down upon close examination. The stratification of society into classes has never been complete. There are not two general classes, but many, they say, and the interests of some social groups "merge imperceptibly with [those of] the others."

In building the case against Marxism, the critics reject the theory of surplus value on the ground that it does not take into consideration the important part played by capital in creating value. The capitalists deserve the greater share of profits, it is said, because they give leadership and direction to enterprise.

The critics deny that the worker's first obligation is to his international class. On the contrary, they say, his first concern should be for the country of his birth. In times of crisis (for example, in 1914), the workers rally to the defense of their own countries.

To the Marxian contention that socialism is "inevitable," the critics maintain that nothing in historical development is absolutely certain. They declare that the thesis of inevitability makes of history an exact science, which they believe it never has been and cannot possibly be. Moreover, the concept of inevitability fails to take into account the highly accidental factors whose nature it is difficult to prophesy.

The argument goes on today. The cold war is in effect a manifestation of the clash between Marxists and anti-Marxists. The work of Marx and Engels unleashed a storm of opposing ideologies which still occupy the attention of men throughout the world. Both friend and foe regard the *Communist Manifesto* as one of the most effective calls to action ever written.

Sidney Hook gave this clue to an understanding of Marx: [1]

Karl Marx is one of the most influential figures of human history. Judged by the number of those who have regarded themselves his followers, and of the organizations set up by them, he has inspired the greatest mass movement of all times. This movement transcends national, racial, and continental boundaries. . . . In some regions . . . of the world, a new religion has arisen which proclaims that History is God and Karl Marx its chief prophet.

---

[1] Sidney Hook, *The Ambiguous Legacy: Marx and the Marxists*, (Princeton, N.J., 1955), p. 11.

THE OPENING OF JAPAN, 1853

"They have measured the ships, guns,
and every odd and end they can spy."

THE HISTORY of Japan is a fascinating story of the transformation of a closed society into a world power. The early Japanese were organized in independent clans, each ruled by a priest-chieftain. Japanese folklore refers to the first emperor of Japan as Jimmu Tenno, who was descended from the Sun Goddess and who became emperor in 660 B.C. His family ruled Japan in the longest unbroken line in world history. The dynasty stemmed from the most important tribal group, the Yamato clan, living on Honshu. The Yamato began to extend their control over other clans.

The original religion of Japan was Shinto (the Divine Way of the Gods), a mixture of nature and ancestor worship. Following are its main tenets:

— The Sun Goddess is the divine ancestress of the Yamato and, eventually, of all the Japanese people.

— The Emperor is divine because he is the extension of the Sun Goddess.

— Japan is under the special guardianship of the gods. The Japanese are virtuous, being descended from the gods. Their soil and institutions are unique and superior to all others.

— The dead are ghosts living in a world of darkness but able to bring sorrow or joy into the lives of the living.

— It is Japan's mission to "bring the whole world under one roof."

Agriculture was the basis of the early economy. Clan rulers and nobles owned the land. Below them in the social scale were farmers and artisans, and at the bottom were serfs and slaves. Warrior nobles held high status.

During the Han dynasty, Chinese culture was transmitted to Japan from Korea. Merchants brought silkworms; scholars brought Chinese script and the riches of Chinese literature to Japan. Buddhism, introduced in the sixth century A.D., was opposed by conservative Japanese, but it gained a foothold and attracted many converts.

In 646 A.D. the Taikwa Reform document elevated the ruler to Supreme Monarch, who held political, military, and religious control over the people. Rebellion against the divine Emperor was looked upon as a religious crime. Instead of local tribal units, imperial administration took over. There was a highly regarded civil service, to which entry was made by examination. All important posts were held by high nobles and the offices were hereditary.

In the eighth century A.D. the illustrious Fujiwara family rose to power, dominating not only the imperial government at the new capital of Kyoto, but also the provinces. Little by little the Fujiwaras reduced the Emperor to a puppet ruler. On more than one occasion they forced a royal son to retire to a Buddhist monastery while one of their family ruled the country. It became customary for the Empress to be chosen from among its members. The Fujiwaras gave Japan many scholars and statesmen. Eventually, they were unable to control the rising disorder. To protect their estates they hired bands of professional soldiers.

A feudal society began to emerge after a struggle for power among the warrior families of Taira and Minamoto. In 1185 the Taira were finally exterminated. In this struggle Yorimoto (1147-1199), chief of the Minamoto, was the victor and reigned under the title of Sai-Tai-Shogun (Barbarian-Subduing-Generalissimo) with the right to nominate his own successor. As *shogun* (military leader), Yorimoto was the real ruler of Japan. He appointed constables and land stewards in each province to discourage rebellion, and collected estate rents as a tax for the support of the military. His military organization, call the *bakafu*, was to last for seven centuries.

Military dictator Yorimoto died in 1199, whereupon the family of Hojo, which had been his stewards, took over the reins of power, using the same Fujiwara technique of governing in the name of puppet *shoguns*. By this time the *samurai* the warrior caste, became influential. The provincial clans finally won great power under the shogunate. The caste was distinct from the ordinary nobles (*kuge*) and from the common people.

During the Hojo period, official recognition was given to *bushido*. the unwritten code of honor of the *samurai*. Similar to European chivalry, *bushido* originated in the twelfth century. Its main principles were simplicity, courage, loyalty, justice, and composure. It approved the custom of *seppuku* – ceremonial suicide, known in the West as *hara-kiri*. By taking his own life with a sword, a warrior could escape the disgraceful crime of "losing face." In the thirteenth and fourteenth centuries, *bushido* took on elements of Zen Buddhism, a cult calling for unusual mental concentration and an ascetic way of life, and appealing especially to the warrior class.

The most important event of the Hojo era was the repulse of an invasion from

Mongol China. The conqueror, Kublai Khan, hearing reports about the wealth of Japan, decided to absorb the string of islands. After an unsuccessful expedition in 1274, he tried again in 1281, this time with 150,000 men and 3,500 ships. The vast fleet was hit by disaster. While the Mongol army was dispersed on the shores, its ships were smashed by a terrific tempest since known as *kamikaze,* or "The Great Wind."

Hojo power was weakened by the Mongol invasion. A quarrel about the succession rose again, after which a cadet branch of the Monamoto family, the Ashikaga, won the title of *shogun.* In 1333 Emperor Go-Diago was forced to abdicate and fled, pursued by the soldiers of Ashikaga Takauji. The latter set up the Asikaga shogunate, which held power until 1565. During this time the Japanese learned that their islands were close enough to the mainland for commercial and cultural contact, but far enough away to be immune to further attack. There was to be no successful invasion of Japan until 1945.

This was the story of a closed society, which wanted nothing more than to be left alone by the rest of the world. Yet, Japan was destined to be opened to the West in an important turning point of history.

March 31, 1854 — December 7, 1941. These dates marked the beginning and end of a tragic cycle in Japanese-American relations.

Bewiskered Commodore Perry ("Old Matt" to his crews), anchored his "black ships of evil mien" in the Bay of Tokyo in the summer of 1853. At long last the door to Japan was opened by Westerners. The Dutch had already been there on the mainland, only to meet the opposition of Japanese who objected to the Dutch way of carrying on business as unnecessarily humiliating.

Before Perry's day, Yankee sea captains defied the boycott, but nevertheless found it impossible to raise the bamboo curtain. George Cleveland, who had landed goods in Japan as early as 1801, reported: "No person in this country (who has not traded with people who have so little intercourse with the world), can have an idea of the trouble we had in delivering the little invoice." Visiting one of their towns, he noted: "At the end of every street is a gate, which is locked at night — and if a citizen were to pass the night in any other than his own street, his name would be taken by the person who keeps the gate, and most probably handed to the Police Officer."

Near the modern city of Yokohama a great scene was played out as the Japanese bowed to Perry. Another momentous drama was enacted by a similar cast aboard the *Missouri* in 1945. The Japanese yielded on both occasions to superior force and scientific ingenuity. They were quick to learn. Perry, later praised by the Nipponese, taught them a technique which they used in imposing a similar treaty on Korea in 1876.

A young naval officer, Edward Yorke McCauley, was an eyewitness to the extraordinary mission. In his *Diary* he left an account of the visits to Naha on Okinawa in August 1853, and of the events surrounding the signing of the treaty on March 31, 1854. Of special interest is McCauley's account of the fantastic espionage practiced by the Japanese, both toward foreigners and toward their own people. Beneath the mask of bowing, scraping, and politeness was hidden an extraordinarily suspicious people.

August 20th [1853]. We walked through the town of Naha. The streets are all paved with granite, cut in all manners of shapes, with the edges neatly fitting each other. The houses are low, and the tiles cemented together presenting a very tidy appearance. Every house is walled around seven or eight feet high, and none have a direct entrance, but by zigzag path round little walls and fences, which, though very good for the purpose of keeping off the spy, upon which system the government is founded, suggests difficulties in getting an easy access home after partaking of the compliments of the season on a New Year's day, and in no way reconcilable with the object of latch keys.

Their dress consists of a short pair of "what d'ye call 'ems' "(unmens): something like a ballet mistress's (not visible at all times, but chiefly so in windy weather and trotting up and down on board of ship), and a garment built of linen; blue or brown, like a Jew's gaberdine. Their hair is shaved on the crown of the head leaving a band of hair about three inches wide which is gathered up into a neat little knot on the top of their pates and secured with a couple of skillets. The hair in doing this is drawn very taut, and when their toilet is over they walk along with the air of saying, "I'm ready for any emergency. I'm pointed at the end, ready for a transit even through an eyebolt." They patronize very large bamboo umbrellas roofed with Japanned paper, rattan sandals, and are altogether an inoffensively clean people, with nothing coffin-ny about them.

We walked leisurely along the road to Thoudi, all paved in the same regular way. I should suppose that those roads are nearly of Deluvian date, from their length and number. As we walked along, we became painfully aware of the fact of our being under the surveillance of the police. There was a spy ahead and another astern, and as fast as we went they kept on in their stations. If any laborers happened to be coming along the road they passed the word to them and down they would squat with their backs toward us until we passed. Shops shut up, women disappeared, as though we were a "marriage blight," and children nearly went into fits in their terror and haste to get out of sight. If we dodged the van and rear spies and made a dip into a bye lane, a mandarin had apparently done so a moment before us, quite accidentally, of course, and everybody was seen helter skelter at the bottom of the street for a moment, and then vanish, leaving everything private and marketable where it stood.

This state of affairs not pleasing the Medico, and disagreeing entirely with my state of mind, we resolved to let them have their own way, and at the same time give them a little exercise, in view of which we separated with the intention of meeting at the opposite end of the town under the walls of the Palace. Then commenced a series of dodgings, counter-marchings, weatherings and sidling offs. I would walk ahead ten paces or so, and then go about and dash down an alley through doors, making a shell of myself in a family circle, shaking hands, patting everbody on the head, now getting into a schoolhouse conciliating the brats (easily done), now in a Pagoda, telegraphing eternal amity with the Bonzes, and bumping my pate in honor of Jos, according to their directions, which so gratified them (like all other Bonzes, having an eye to proselytism) that they tea'd and smoked me before the mandarins had the smallest idea of my geographical position. And off again into a silversmith's; out again before he could pantomime "tea," knocking down an accidental mandarin in my hurry to get through the town before the Medico anatomized the interior of the market basket without me.

The system of spying here is carried out not only on strangers arriving here, who are requested to clear out as soon as possible, but also among themselves, every man being a spy on his neighbor, so that everything that passes is known to the mandarins, who generally, I believe, are sent here from Japan, and are exceedingly jealous of everything they have. So that the moment one of us put their foot ashore, shops are closed and everything likely to interest us is put out of sight. With the islanders in general, we are great favorites. They come on board, will take anything to eat confidently, whereas on shore they will not touch it. It is true they are all the time so scared with the guns, drums, and calls as to be enjoying a somewhat precarious existence, but when they go they grin with satisfaction and always manage to come a second time in spite of the mandarins, who never if they can help it allow the same crew to come twice lest they should be conciliated and always have them accompanied by one of their own order.

Feb. 17th: [The] Commodore, having given the natives three days to decide on giving him a reception here or at Jeddo, they came on board today in a glorious humor, saying that they had good news from Jeddo; that the treaty was to be signed and everything settled amicably. I even got a pair of the officials to come down into the steerage, where we gave them a little feed, and a glass of something to astonish their insides. But, bless my wig, they swallowed poteen, brandy, gin and saki alternately, a mixture that would swamp the d − vl himself; and finally went off as happy as two such polite beings could ever get. (It wasn't the first time that party got drunk by a long shot!) Before leaving, they showed us their swords, which are certainly beautiful. The grasp is long enough to be held by both hands and something to spare.

One thing must be said of these people, which cannot be gainsaid, that they are without exception the most polite people on the face of the earth, not only on board here, but also in their boats alongside. Their intercourse with one another seemed to be of the most amiable and self-denying kind. This affects even their gestures. They are very graceful in everything except walking, which their garments deforms into a waddle. They are very inquisitive about everything on board. They have measured the ship, guns, and every odd and end they can spy.

March 27th [1854]: Fitted out the quarterdeck with flags, and all sorts of contrivances usual on such occasions, as bayonet, chandeliers, musket rack, candlesticks, etc., etc.

A table was set below for the Commodore and the high Commissioners, and another on deck for the lesser gents and the officers of the Squadron. This arrangement was consequent to the fact that the smaller fry are not allowed to sit, or eat in the presence of their Princes. At three their barge went alongside of the Macedonian, where they were shown around and saluted with seventeen guns on leaving. They then came on board here. Steam was up on one boiler. The engine was turned and explained. Every one of them had his paper and pencil at hand, and copied everything they could get at. One of the field pieces was worked with blank cartridges, quite surprising them by the rapidity with which they are fired. Afterwards they adjourned to dinner. Of course it was my luck to have the deck and I lost all the best part of the fun, being relieved about dessert time.

I had an opportunity of joining in a toast or two, and a peep at the state of affairs. The seats round the board were filled alternately with Japanese and Americans. The ladies of the respective lands were toasted and cheered with great good will. I am sorry to say that I perceived some of the two parties telegraphing the intention of a reciprocal interchange of sweethearts. Of course, they were laboring under the influence of the friendly spirits of the times.

As soon as the eating was over, a new phase took place. Every Japanese (except the interpreters who had learnt better by their acquaintance with Dutch and finding out from books what our customs are) left their seats and commenced pocketing all the edibles they could lay their hands on, wrapping each piece of pie, slice of beef, leg of chicken, etc., in a piece of paper, depositing it in the bag of their capacious sleeves. It was laughable to see them trotting around the tables picking out whatever suited their fancies. I saw one character end his foray by emptying a saltcellar. White sugar and cut glass are their particular weakness.

When the dinner was over the Commodore and party came on deck and all proceeded to the main deck, where a stage had been arranged for an Ethiopian performance. This they enjoyed very much, laughing violently during the whole exhibition. Some of them, were very much affected by champagne, but none lost their dignity of manner for a moment, except one old fellow, who, it is said, is a habitual toper, and was caught learning the Polka from a midshipman on the hurricane deck. At sunset they left.

[March] 31st, Today the treaty was signed in great style, but being laid up [with scurvy], I am unable to go and see the instrument before it is boxed up. It appears that the port of Simoda in the principality of Idzu, Hakodaté in the principality of Matsumai, and Napa-Kiang in the Loochoo group are to be thrown open to us at once, or rather within the next fifty days, and that in the course of five years, when they have gained, as they say, a little more experience in the way of foreign trade, they will throw more ports open.

The Japanese were delighted when Perry showed them a model telegraph and a model railway. They began to recognize the folly of isolating themselves from the progress of Western countries. They agreed to Perry's demand for American trade and a guarantee of safety for shipwrecked sailors. Perry's deed and the later awakening of the country led to the downfall of the shogunate.

Perry's feat in opening Japan was followed by a grand scramble for privileges. European powers quickly sought treaties and extraterritorial privileges. When conservative Japanese elders protested against foreign penetration, they were taught a lesson in Western fashion by the bombardment of the town of Shimonoseki

(1863). The Japanese concluded intelligently that Western military, political, and economic methods were far more effective than their own. Thereafter, being both adaptable and fanatically nationalistic, in contrast with the disunited Chinese, they resisted Western imperialism, and even used Western methods to develop an imperialism of their own.

The rapid Westernization of Japan is one of the most remarkable phenomena of modern times. Virtually overnight, the whole structure of Japanese society was transformed from top to bottom. In 1867 the young *mikado* Mutsuhito, wrested power from the *shogun,* and during the rest of his very long reign, instituted reforms which changed feudal Japan into a modern constitutional state, an industrial nation, and a world power.

Feudalism was abolished in 1871, and the land was divided among independent farmers. In 1872 came the opening of the first railroad and the introduction of compulsory elementary education. Universal military service (under German direction), and the construction of a modern navy (under British guidance) followed soon after. There were many more reforms: students were sent to foreign countries to study Western culture and science; new codes of civil and criminal law were drafted; religious liberty was established; and trade and industry were promoted by the government so effectively that Japan became a dynamic industrial power. In 1889 the *mikado* promulgated a constitution providing for a parliament of two houses, although he retained the right of veto.

Compared with the transformation of Japan, the industrialization of England was positively snail-like. The Japanese accomplished in approximately a quarter of a century an evolution for which Europe had taken some five thousand years. The Western nations were astonished to find in Japan a real commercial rival, one which was able to compete successfully with them in the markets of the world.

As an industrial power Japan, like the European imperialist countries, required colonies, markets, raw materials, areas in which to invest surplus capital, and an outlet for her surplus population. Regarding herself as the protector and guardian of Oriental civilization, she turned to China — the slumbering giant already in process of dismemberment

Russia now looked upon Japan as her rival in the Far East, while the Japanese were angered by a series of Russian successes. The Russians had obtained the right to extend the Chinese Eastern Railway to Vladivostok. They leased the Liao-tung peninsula and Port Arthur, and penetrated Korea and Manchuria. When Japan demanded that Russia withdraw from Manchuria and Korea, the pygmy and the giant made ready for a deadly struggle. The Russo-Japanese War (1904—1905), to the amazement of the entire world, ended in the rout of the Russian armies at Mukden and the destruction of a Russian fleet at Tsushima. Russia turned out to be a giant with feet of clay. Peace was concluded in the Treaty of Portsmouth (New Hampshire) in 1905. Both parties agreed to leave Manchuria, but each retained spheres of influence there. Japan won Port Arthur, a lease on the Liao-tung peninsula, and the southern half of the island of Sakhalin. Japanese influence was recognized in Korea.

It was an astonishing climb for the people of Nippon. When "Old Matt" Perry opened Japan to the West, he was — without knowing it — changing the power structure of the world.

AFRICA: STANLEY MEETS LIVINGSTONE, 1871

"Dr. Livingstone, I presume?"

THE OPENING of Japan was one phase of a worldwide phenomenon — the revival of imperialism. The urge toward expansion has always been present in Europe. In the early modern era the old imperialism arose concomitantly with the Commercial Revolution and the discovery of the New World. Spain, Holland, Portugal, France, and England founded colonial empires and Europeanized the Americas. During the waves of imperialism the interests of the colonies were regarded as subservient to those of the mother country — an accurate reflection of the mercantilism of the day.

This early aggressive urge eventually subsided. Enthusiasm for acquiring colonies abated with the end of the First French Colonial Empire in 1763, the decline of the First British Empire in 1783, and the loss of South America by Spain and Portugal in the early 1820's. Critics decried the quest for colonies as wasted effort. In any case, the energy of European peoples was spent in the French Revolution, the Napoleonic Wars, and the subsequent European struggles between reaction and democracy. After the defeat of Napoleon there remained but one strong colonial empire of any consequence — the British. For more than half a century after 1815 there were no important colonial rivalries.

Suddenly, in the decade after 1870, there was another great turning point in a revival of imperialism, a new era of overseas expansion. On the pretext of Europeanizing backward peoples, the imperialist nations engaged in a wild scramble for rich territories in Africa, Asia, and the Near and Middle East. Once again the mainstream of world history changed course.

Behind this movement there were many motives. The imperial powers were influenced by different combinations of goals, but the basic drive was economic. The New Industrial Revolution impelled country after country into the machine age. Growing industrialization called for new markets, sources of raw materials to feed the insatiable iron monsters — the machines, more food for increased populations, and new fields for investing excess capital. European life required many products which only tropical regions could supply. The desire of industrial countries to sell their own products in new markets was essentially a revival of the mercantilism of the eighteenth century. Money invested in "backward" countries would bring a higher rate of return than if used at home.

A second motive for the new expansionism was psychological. National self-consciousness entered an acute stage by the last quarter of the nineteenth century. Poets and historians began to talk about "the historic mission of expansion." Nationalism merged into imperialism; both were saturated with the same romanticism and mysticism. There was loud talk about "a place in the sun," "the white man's burden," "manifest destiny," and "the lamp of life." Germany and Italy, each now unified and both envious of British and French colonial successes, began to look for new worlds to conquer. Colonies were valuable, it was said, for "excess population," even though ironically, comparatively few people would migrate to the colonies.

Another motive was religious — the urge to spread Christianity. Both Catholic and Protestant missionaries went out to convert nonbelievers. True — the missionaries themselves were moved by religious and humanitarian ideals, but these altruistic men of God were cruelly used by imperialists bent on gaining entry to new and valuable regions. When an overzealous missionary violated native customs and as a result had to pay the price of his life, a handy pretext was created for aggression. Imperialism was sparked by other ideals than mere justice.

This was the milieu. How did imperialism start in Africa, the great dark continent? There are five Africas, not one. The northern coastline, bordering the Mediterranean, is a temperate area that historically has been an adjunct of European civilization. Just south of this area is the belt of the Sahara, Libyan, and Nubian deserts, where the white and Negro racial strains begin to blend. The next belt stretches across the continent from Guinea to the Sudan, the so-called "land of the blacks." Next there is Central, or Equatorial, Africa, land of dense jungles, inhabited by Negroes. And at the southern tip of the great continent is again a temperate zone in the area around South Africa.

European nations had only small footholds on this great continent. The Portuguese, French, and British had coastal trading posts of their own, but none had penetrated into the interior of the continent. Interest in Africa had been stimulated in the early nineteenth century by the stories of missionaries, traders and adventurers. But the great trek to the dark continent did not begin until the last third of the nineteenth century.

In March 1866 a Scottish explorer-missionary, David Livingstone, landed on the shore of East Africa near the mouth of the river Rovuma. Shortly thereafter he disappeared in the bush. From that time until he died in 1873 at a remote African village seven hundred miles from the coast, only one white man was to see him again. Livingstone's explorations in Africa had a double purpose — to find the source of the Nile and to bring the slave trade to an end. Arab traders had moved into the heart of the continent, not only to obtain copper and ivory, but also to seize men, women, and children as slaves. "I have been led on from one step to another," Livingstone declared, "by the overruling providence of the great Parent," in order to achieve "a great good for Africa."

Responsible for that spark which opened Africa was James Gordon Bennett, Jr., the proprietor of *The New York Herald*, who commissioned one of his star reporters to equip an expedition to search for the lost explorer. The man to whom he turned was Henry Morton Stanley. Born in North Wales in 1841, the son of a cottager, Stanley was reared in a workhouse, shipped as a cabin boy to New Orleans, and enrolled as a volunteer in the Confederate Army. Taken prisoner at Shiloh, he managed his release from prison camp by enlisting in a Federal artillery unit.

In his best-selling travel book, *How I Found Livingstone* (1872), Stanley tells the circumstances surrounding his assignment. Summoned to Bennett's quarters at the Grand Hotel in Paris on October 16, 1869, he learned from his chief that he was to lead an expedition to find the missing explorer. "Draw a thousand pounds now," said Bennett, "and when you have gone through that, draw another thousand, and when that is spent, draw another thousand, and so on, but *find Livingstone!*"

Stanley's expedition from Zanzibar into the interior of Africa turned out to be a high point in African exploration. The meeting of reporter and explorer at Ujiji on November 10, 1871, was one of the great journalistic scoops of history. In the story of the incident Stanley maintained a sense of high adventure, excitement, and tension. The following extracts are from his report in *The New York Herald,* August 10, 1872.

BUNDER UJIJI,[1] ON LAKE TANGANYIKA, CENTRAL AFRICA, NOVEMBER 23, 1871 — Only two months gone, and what a change in my feelings! But two months ago, what a peevish, fretful soul was mine! What a hopeless prospect presented itself before your correspondent! Arabs vowing that I would never behold Tanganyika; Sheik, the son of Nahib, declaring me a madman to his fellows because I would not heed his words. My own men deserting, my servants whining day by day, and my white man endeavoring to impress me with the belief that they were all doomed men! And the only answer to it all is Livingstone, the hero traveler, is alongside of me, writing as hard as he can to his friends in England, India, and America, and I am quite safe and sound in health and limb. Wonderful, is it not, that such a thing should be, when the seers had foretold that it would be otherwise — that all my schemes, that all my determination, would avail me nothing? But probably you are in as much of a hurry to know how it all took place as I am to relate. So, to the recital.

---

[1] Anglo-Indian for "harbor."

September 23 I left Unyanyembe, driving before me fifty well-armed black men, loaded with the goods of the expedition, and dragging after me one white man. Several Arabs stood by my late residence to see the last of me and mine, as they felt assured that there was not the least hope of their ever seeing me again. Shaw, the white man, was as pale as death, and would willingly have received the order to stop behind in Unyanyembe, only he had not quite the courage to ask permission, from the fact that only the night before he had expressed a hope that I would not leave him behind, and I had promised to give him a good riding donkey and to walk after him until he recovered perfect health. However, as I gave the order to march, some of the men, in a hurry to obey the order, managed to push by him suddenly and down he went like a dead man. The Arabs, thinking doubtless that I would not go now because my white subordinate seemed so ill, hurried in a body to the fallen man, loudly crying at what they were pleased to term my cruelty and obstinacy; but, pushing them back, I mounted Shaw on his donkey, and told them that I must see Tanganyika first, as I had sworn to go on . . . .

Once away from the hateful valley of Kwihara, once out of sight of the obnoxious fields, my enthusiasm for my work rose as newborn as when I left the coast. But my enthusiasm was short-lived, for before reaching camp I was almost delirious with fever . . . .

Near Isinga met a caravan of eighty Waguha direct from Ujiji, bearing oil, and bound for Unyanyembe. They report that a white man was left by them five days ago at Ujiji. He had the same color as I have, wears the same shoes, the same clothes, and has hair on his face like I have, only his is white. This is Livingstone. Hurrah for Ujiji! My men share my joy, for we shall be coming back now directly; and, being so happy at the prospect, I buy three goats and five gallons of native beer, which will be eaten and drank directly . . . .

We are now about descending — in a few minutes we shall have reached the spot where we imagine the object of our search — our fate will soon be decided. No one in that town knows we are coming; least of all do they know we are so close to them. If any of them ever heard of the white man at Unyanyembe they must believe we are there yet. We shall take them all by surprise, for no other but a white man would dare leave Unyanyembe for Ujiji with the country in such a distracted state — no other but a crazy white man, whom Sheik, the son of Nasib, is going to report to Syed or Prince Burghash for not taking his advice.

Well, we are but a mile from Ujiji now, and it is high time that we let them know that a caravan is coming; so "Commence firing" is the word passed along the length of the column, and gladly do they begin. They have loaded their muskets half full, and they roar like a broadside of a line-of-battle ship. Down go the ramrods, sending huge charges home to the breech, and volley after volley is fired. The flags are fluttered; the banner of America is in front, waving joyfully; the guide is in the zenith of his glory. The former residents of Zanzita will know directly and will wonder — as well they may — as to what it means. Never were the Stars and Stripes so beautiful in my mind — the breeze of the Tanganika has such an effect on them. The guide blows his horn, and the shrill, wild clangor of it is far and near; and still the cannon muskets tell the noisy seconds.

By this time the Arabs are fully alarmed; the natives of Ujiji, Waguha, Warundi, Wanguana, and I know not whom hurry up by the hundreds to ask what it all means — this fusillading, shouting, and blowing of horns and flag flying. There are Yambos shouted out to me by the dozen, and delighted Arabs have run up breathlessly to shake my hand and ask anxiously where I come from. But I have no patience with them. The expedition goes far too slow. I should like to settle the vexed question by one personal view. Where is he? Has he fled?

Suddenly a man — a black man — at my elbow shouts in English, "How do you do, sir?"

"Hello, who the deuce are you?"

"I am the servant of Dr. Livingstone," he says; and before I can ask any more questions he is running like a madman toward the town.

We have at last entered the town. There are hundreds of people around me — I might say thousands without exaggeration, it seems to me. It is a grand triumphal procession. As we move, they move. All eyes are drawn toward us. The expedition at last comes to a halt; the journey is ended for a time; but I alone have a few more steps to make.

There is a group of the most respectable Arabs, and as I come nearer I see the white face of an old man among them. He has a cap with a gold band around it, his dress is a short jacket of red blanket cloth, and his pants — well, I didn't observe. I am shaking hands with him. We raise our hats, and I say:

"Dr. Livingstone, I presume?"

And he says, "Yes."

Finis coronat opus. [2]

Livingstone's explorations in the regions of the Congo River, Lake Tanganyika, and Northern Rhodesia, and Stanley's exciting stories of pygmies, Amazons, cannibals, exotic animals, rubber-producing plants, and other wonders of the Dark Continent precipitated an undignified scramble for Africa among the Great Powers. Fired with ambition, hundreds of explorers hit the African trail.

Meanwhile, exploration went on at an increased pace. The sources of the Nile were explored by Burton, Speke, Baker, Schweinfurth, and Grant; the Sahara and Sudan by Nachtigal, Barth, Laing, and Denham; the Niger by Caillé, Clapperton, and Lander; the Zambesi valley by Livingstone; the Congo by Stanley and de Brazza. Europe turned its eyes to possibilities for commerce and missionary work.

By this time the process was a familiar one. A small group of white men — explorers, traders, promoters — would appear in the wilderness, bringing with them a handful of treaties, sometimes merely printed forms. They would seek out a native chief who appeared to have some influence over his people and bestow powers on him which he ordinarily did not possess — such as the right to convey sovereignty, sell land, or grant concessions. Thus, control was gained indirectly

---

[2] "The end crowns the work."

through tribal chieftains. Then came what amounted to forced labor and exploitation of the area. Money was the root of evil in this Valhalla.

In 1876 Leopold II (1835-1909), King of the Belgians, organized a commercial company to exploit Central Africa. The Great Powers reluctantly consented to the formation of Leopold's Congo Free State, from which the Belgian ruler acquired an enormous fortune (rubber and ivory). But Leopold's unscrupulous treatment of the natives aroused such indignation that the Congo Free State was abolished in 1908. The region was annexed to Belgium as the Belgian Congo.

The major European powers, while assuring the world that their object was merely to "Christianize and civilize" the Negroes, rushed in to acquire the natural resources of "Dark Africa." The natives, too weak to protest, offered their lands and their freedom in exchange for work, taxes, exploitation, and death. It was not long before almost the entire continent was partitioned among the European powers.

Working quietly, efficiently, and with tone, tact, and taste, the British acquired the lion's share. Already holding Cape Colony (ceded by the Netherlands in 1815 at the Congress of Vienna), Britain seized Egypt in 1882 and, in 1899, established virtual sovereignty over the Anglo-Egyptian Sudan. After the discovery of gold and diamonds in South Africa, Britain made war on the Dutch settlers (Boer War, 1899-1902), and eventually won the whole of South Africa. In the west she acquired the Gold Coast, Nigeria, Sierra Leone, and the lower Gambian region. In East Africa she annexed Uganda, Kenya, and a part of Somaliland.

The French refused to be left out. They got a foothold in Algeria as early as 1830, then gradually extended their control into Morocco and Tunis along the Mediterranean coast, and annexed most of northwest Africa from Algeria south to the Congo River. In East Africa, France acquired a part of Somaliland and the island of Madagascar.

Some were left behind in the wild scramble. Germany was a late starter in the African hunt, but she was able to obtain a number of vacant areas, such as the Cameroons, Togoland, German South West Africa, and German East Africa. These were good-sized splotches on the map, but they were poor in natural resources, leftovers in the scramble. To that disappointment was added German resentment against accusations of brutality in handling the natives.

Following her unification, Italy sought new prestige as well as economic enhancement by annexing Eritrea and Italian Somaliland, both coastal districts in East Africa. When she sought to acquire Abyssinia (Ethiopia), Italy was halted with a crushing defeat at Adowa (1896). But she managed to wrest Tripoli and Cyrenaica from the Turks. The Italians claimed population pressure as an additional motive for expansion.

Portugal, as her share of the spoils, obtained Angola, Portuguese Guinea, and Portuguese East Africa. Spain took Rio de Oro on the extreme west coast, the northern coast of Morocco, and a few small islands off the coast.

It was necessary to find some justification for what amounted to bare aggression.

In 1884 the Great Powers met in Berlin and in 1885 issued the Berlin Act to lay down rules for expansion in Africa. The signatories promised "to protect the natives in their moral and material well-being, to co-operate in the suppression of slavery and the slave trade, to further the education and civilization of the natives, to protect missionaries and explorers." But the signatories also agreed that occupation of African lands must not be on paper only, and that a power with holdings on the coast had prior rights in the back country. The intentions were good, but the opportunity was lost to prevent greedy land grabbing. Profits came first, the well-being of the natives a poor second.

Within fifteen years after the Berlin Conference all Africa was parceled out. The only exceptions were Ethiopia and Liberia, the latter founded in 1822 as a colony for emancipated American slaves.

With a bland display of innocence the imperialist powers squeezed the continent of its wealth and at the same time announced to an indifferent world that as do-gooders they were suppressing slavery, tribal warfare, superstition, and disease. Africa could not be left to the lazy natives, any more than the Americas could be retained by backward Indians. This was dead land without Western brains to use it. It was the white man's burden to save the continent for civilization. Are we not bringing education to ignorant natives? Are we not playing light on the Dark Continent?

To these arguments the anti-imperialists countered that little more was done than to drain the colonies of their wealth, and in return the natives were given huge supplies of gin and doses of syphilis. As so often in history, might was right.

The argument went on, but it was clear that the colonizers were mostly interested in gold, rubber, diamonds, ivory, ebony, copra, cocoa, palm oil, cotton, and nuts. The Europeans knew it, and the exploited were aware of it. In the mid-twentieth century, the natives of Africa, having their fill of paternalism, turned the tool of nationalism on their occupiers in what amounted to a new turning point in history — this time suffused with additional bitterness and resentment.

FLIGHT OF THE WRIGHT BROTHERS
AT KITTY HAWK, 1903

Twelve seconds that changed the world.

THE TASK of getting from one place to another, how to move fast on land and sea, has always had high priority on the list of human needs. In his day primitive man cast an envious eye on birds sailing majestically and effortlessly through the air. Perhaps the human animal might do the same. In imitative efforts a long line of would-be heroes in varied contraptions jumped off cliffs in dives ending in disaster. Flying looked easy but there were problems.

The Greeks had a word for it in their mythology. Icarus, son of Daedalus, fled on wings to escape the resentment of Minos, but the sun melted the wax that cemented his wings and he crashed into the Aegean Sea to his death. The Renaissance genius Leonardo da Vinci was fascinated by the prospect of flying. Experts say that had he had at his disposal some source of power such as petrol, he would have devoloped a practical flying machine. For centuries men of genius and just ordinary men dreamed of flying, and the dream was to come true in one of the extraordinary turning points of history.

The story of successful flight began in late 1878 when an American father brought home in Dayton, Ohio, a toy helicopter for his two sons, Orville and Wilbur Wright. The lads were deliriously impressed when "instead of falling to the floor it flew across the room till it struck the ceiling, where it fluttered awhile, and then sank to the floor." The boys never forgot that toy, even after they set up a bicycle shop to make a living.

The mechanically minded brothers were fascinated by anything connected with flying — toy helicopters, kites, gliders. They heard about the experiments of Otto Lilienthal, a German, who was killed in 1896 when he lost control of his primitive glider. He had guided and balanced his machine by simply shifting the weight of his body. The Wrights asked a pertinent question — would it be possible to develop a system in which the center of gravity remained constant and the equilibrium of the glider would be maintained by varying the air pressure through adjusting of the angle of the wings?

The brothers found that virtually all the theories then current on aerodynamics had no validity. In their own experimental wind tunnel they discovered basic facts about lift and drag of air foils. They spent hour after hour experimenting, observing, fixing, and changing. Lifelong bachelors, they had plenty of time for their avocation. After a day's work in the bicycle shop, they would hasten to the wind tunnel in pursuit of their dream.

Eventually, the Wrights produced a model which appeared to be promising. It was crude, but it indicated possible success. Where Lilienthal had balanced his glider in flight by simply shifting his own weight, the Wright brothers used a system of control that kept balance by varying air pressure in different parts of their machine. They wanted a model whose performance could be predicted in advance.

After much experimentation the brothers built a machine designed to be flown as a kite in winds of about fifteen miles an hour. At first they tried flying the machine without a man on board, operating the levers by cords controlled from the ground, a preliminary step toward the great goal.

By late 1903 the brothers had a power-driven craft with a wing span of thirty-three feet. There was a small twelve-horsepower engine with a four-cylinder gasoline motor — the whole contraption weighing 745 pounds. They bought cotton cloth from a department store to form the sails of the double wings. There were no wheels, but instead skids such as those commonly used on snow sleds. To test their machine they brought it to Kill Devil Hill, near Kitty Hawk, on the barrier reefs off the North Carolina coast, where heavy winds roared in south of Cape Hatteras. The critical need was for wind to lift the plane's wings.

On the reef the Wrights constructed a crude monorail track to assist the take-off. Only a few people were present on that historic day of December 17, 1903.

A few days before, on December 8, Samuel P. Langley, the secretary of the Smithsonian Institute and the best known among Americans interested in aviation, had plunged into the Potomac River below Washington in a power-driven airplane that he had built at a cost of $70,000. Dozens of newsmen saw Langley's failure; none was present at the scene of the Wright's triumph. The only newspaper in America to give the flight serious coverage was the Norfolk *Virginian-Pilot*. The reporter tried to sell it first to other papers, but found them too skeptical to buy it. The account, reprinted in part below, appeared in the issue of December 18, 1903, the morning after the successful flights at Kitty Hawk.

The problem of aerial navigation without the use of a balloon has been solved at last.

Over the sand hills of the North Carolina coast yesterday, near Kitty Hawk, two Ohio men proved that they could soar through the air in a flying machine of their own construction, with the power to steer and speed it at will.

This, too, in the face of a wind blowing at the registered velocity of twenty-one miles an hour.

Like a monster bird, the invention hovered above the breakers and circled over the rolling sand hills at the command of its navigator and, after soaring for three miles, it gracefully descended to earth again, and rested lightly upon the spot selected by the man in the car as a suitable landing place.

While the United States government has been spending thousands of dollars in an effort to make practicable the ideas of Professor Langley, of the Smithsonian Institute, Wilbur and Orville Wright, two brothers, natives of Dayton, Ohio, have, quietly, even secretly, perfected their invention and put it to a successful test.

They are not yet ready that the world should know the methods they have adopted in conquering the air, but the *Virginian-Pilot* is able to state authentically the nature of their invention, its principles and its chief dimensions.

The idea of the box kite has been adhered to strictly in the basic formation of the flying machine.

A huge framework of light timbers, thirty-three feet wide, five feet deep, and five feet across the top, forms the machine proper.

This is covered with a tough, but light canvas.

In the center, and suspended just below the bottom plane, is the small gasoline engine which furnished the motive power for the propelling and elevating wheels.

These are two six-bladed propellers, one arranged just below the center of the frame, so gauged as to exert an upward force when in motion, and the other extends horizontally to the rear from the center of the car, furnishing the forward impetus.

Protruding from the center of the car is a huge, fan-shaped rudder of canvas, stretched upon a frame of wood. This rudder is controlled by the navigator and may be moved to each side, raised, or lowered.

Wilbur Wright, the chief inventor of the machine, sat in the operator's car, and when all was ready his brother unfastened the catch which held the invention at the top of the slope.

The big box began to move slowly at first, acquiring velocity as it went, and when halfway down the hundred feet the engine was started.

The propeller in the rear immediately began to revolve at a high rate of speed, and when the end of the incline was reached the machine shot out into space without a perceptible fall.

By this time the elevating propeller was also in motion, and keeping its altitude, the machine slowly began to go higher and higher until it finally soared sixty feet above the ground.

Maintaining this height by the action of the under wheel, the navigator increased the revolutions of the rear propeller, and the forward speed of the huge affair increased until a velocity of eight miles was attained.

All this time the machine headed into a twenty-one-mile wind.

The little crowd of fisherfolk and coast guards, who have been watching the construction of the machine with unconcealed curiosity since September, were amazed.

They endeavored to race over the sand and keep up with the thing in the air, but it soon distanced them and continued its flight alone, save the man in the car.

Steadily it pursued its way, first tacking to port, then to starboard, and then driving straight ahead.

"It is a success," declared Orville Wright to the crowd on the beach after the first mile had been covered.

But the inventor waited. Not until he had accomplished three miles, putting the machine through all sorts of maneuvers en route, was he satisfied.

Then he selected a suitable place to land and, gracefully circling, drew his invention slowly to the earth, where it settled, like some big bird, in the chosen spot.

"Eureka!" he cried, as did the alchemists of old.

The success of the Wright brothers in their invention is the result of three years of hard work. Experiment after experiment has been made and failure resulted, but each experiment had its lesson, and finally, when the two reappeared at Kitty Hawk last fall, they felt more confident than ever. The spot selected for the building and perfecting of the machine is one of the most desolate upon the Atlantic seaboard. Just on the southern extremity of that coast stretch known as the graveyard of American shipping, cut off from civilization by a wide expanse of sound water and seldom in touch with the outer world save when a steamer once or twice a week touches at the little wharf to take and leave government mail, no better place could scarcely have been selected to maintain secrecy.

And this is where the failures have grown into success.

The machine which made yesterday's flight easily carried the weight of a man of 150 pounds, and is nothing like so large as the ill-fated Buzzard of Potomac River Fame.

It is said the Wright bothers intend constructing a much larger machine, but before this they will go back to their homes for the holidays.

Wilbur Wright, the inventor, is a well-groomed man of prepossessing appearance. He is about five feet, six inches tall, weighs about 150 pounds, and is of swarthy complexion. His hair is raven-hued and straight, but a piercing pair of deep-blue eyes peer at you over a nose of extreme length and sharpness.

His brother, Orville, on the other hand, is a blond, with sandy hair and fair complexion, even features, and sparkling black eyes. He is not quite as large as Wilbur, but is of magnificent physique.

The pair have spent almost the entire fall and winter and early spring months of the past three years at Kitty Hawk, working upon their invention, leaving when the weather began to grow warm and returning in the early fall to work.

Their last appearance was on September 1, and since then they have been actively engaged upon the construction of the machine which made yesterday's successful flight.

Most of the story was correct, but actually there were four flights and none was of three miles' duration. Orville Wright made the first flight at 10:30 a.m. The motor was run for a few minutes and then the wire holding the machine to the monorail was released. The plane dashed forward with Wilbur Wright running at the side holding the wing to balance the craft on the track (there is a famous news photograph of this great moment). The plane stayed in the air at ten feet for just twelve seconds — twelve of the most extraordinary seconds in the story of mankind. Then it made an erratic descent just 120 feet from the point at which it was air-borne.

The second and third flights were just a little longer. The fourth and final flight came at noon when Wilbur Wright covered 852 feet and remained in the air fifty-nine seconds. Then a sudden gust of wind turned the plane over and damaged the power plant. The brothers decided to call it a day — but what a day!

Those were slow, awkward hops, but they meant the realization of one of man's oldest dreams.

At first there was little recognition. Critics were certain that the brothers were lunatics, and even their father was inclined to laugh at them. Wilbur Wright died of typhoid fever in 1912. Orville, chagrined by disputes on the priority of his flight, angrily retired. In 1928 he removed the original plane from the Smithsonian Institute in Washington and presented it to a London museum. After his death in 1948, the plane was returned to Washington.

During World War II Orville Wright was asked if he was sorry that he had invented the first flying machine. "No," he replied, "I feel about it much as I do about fire. I regret its damage but I am glad the human race discovered it."

That one-thousand-dollar flying machine was just the start. Design followed design in continuous progress. The tiny craft may be compared with the marvel of engineering which has led to the Boeing 747, the current superjet liner which has revolutionized travel by air. Statistics on the new $21-million plane defy the imagination. It is so big that the Wrights could have made their twelve-second, 120-foot maiden flight in about half the length of its fuselage. It weighs 350 tons, with a wing span of 195 feet. There are spacious lounges and a stairway to the upper deck. The pilots sit in a cabin three stories high, and the tail is as tall as a five-story apartment building. Four great turbines with 43,500 pounds of thrust each (about 20,000 horsepower) push the giant plane through the skies. The 375 passengers cruise at 625 miles per hour, enjoying feature-length movies, or TV-via-communications-satellite. Flight crews use computers for the trips, even landing automatically.

The twelve-second trip of the Wrights and the first flight to the moon were both epochal milestones in scientific and technical progress. An imaginative novelist foresaw both flights: a century ago, Jules Verne, the father of science fiction, wrote about flying machines and described a voyage to the moon by three men in a spacecraft. The Wright brothers and the three American astronauts acted out Jules Verne's stories in real life — with some technical differences.

ASSASSINATION AT SARAJEVO, JUNE 28, 1914

"He uttered only one word , 'Sofia'
– a call to his stricken wife."

THE OPENING of the twentieth century was rich in promise. The triumphs of invention and technology seemed to lift man ever upward to a higher plane. On the credit side were the lengthening of the life span, lessening of physical suffering, increased control of environmental conditions, and conquest of time and space. There was indication that science would promote an infinite extension of comfort and happiness.

Above all was the promise of a peaceful world. For centuries human beings had slaughtered one another in the name of God, religion, or the nation. It seemed that at long last man was using his intelligence to place war in the category to which it belonged – along with cannibalism – and that the new century would see the era of peace on earth.

So it seemed – but the dream was destined to end in nightmare. In two crashing turning points – World Wars I and II – the peoples of the world destroyed one another in tens of millions. It is a tragic story of the inability of humans to avoid the pitfalls of war.

Europe was a camp of potential belligerents, each armed and feverishly preparing for the coming struggle. The introduction of military conscription and the development of new instruments of warfare reflected the mutual distrust of Europeans. Military and naval expenditures in both large and small nations rose enormously during the period from 1872 to 1912. In Germany there was an increase of 335 per cent; in Russia 214 per cent; in France 133 per cent; and in England 180 per cent. The desire for an armed peace imposed a staggering burden on all countries.

Diplomacy was entangled in international anarchy. Although each nation maintained the peace within its own borders by constitutional and legal provisions, the family of Europeans had no restraining overall organization. International relations, based on the principle of national autonomy, permitted each power to act as it thought best in all matters. "International law," a body of rules and regulations supposedly governing intercourse between nations, existed in theory, but in the absence of any supranational authority, offenders were subject only to the "judgment of mankind." Diplomacy became a labyrinth of trickery. Sworn allies were not necessarily loyal friends. In some cases, nations made secret agreements with the enemies of their allies. Attempts were made to construct some kind of international machinery such as the Hague Conferences of 1899 and 1907, but such efforts were sporadic and ineffective. The peace movement was on the verge of collapse.

The climate – economic, political, and diplomatic – was conducive to war, and only a spark was needed to start the conflagration. That came in an obscure city in the Balkans.

Emperor Francis Joseph of Austria-Hungary was one of the unhappiest monarchs who ever sat on a throne. His brother, Maximilian, appointed puppet emperor of Mexico by Louis Napoleon, fell before a firing squad of Mexicans. As a result his sister-in-law, the wife of Maximilian, went insane. In 1889 his only son and heir, Rudolph, either committed suicide or was murdered, together with the prince's young mistress, the Baroness Marie Vetsera, in a hunting lodge at Mayerling, near Vienna. Francis Joseph's wife was killed in 1898 by an anarchist. There seemed to be enough tragedy in the life of the old man.

On Sunday, June 28, 1914, the sorely tried monarch received the news that his nephew and heir to the throne, Francis Ferdinand, and the latter's morganatic wife, Sofia Chotek, had been assassinated at Sarajevo, the capital of Bosnia. The Archduke was on an official visit to preside at army maneuvers, ostensibly to win the loyalty of the peasantry by affording them a glimpse of their future ruler. Serbian terrorists seized the opportunity to murder him.

The assassin, Gavrilo Princip, was a Bosnian Serb, nineteen years of age. As a small boy he had tended sheep on the hills and learned from the highland peasants the old folk songs and tales of Serbia's glorious past. Expelled from the *Gymnasium* at Sarajevo for revolutionary activities, he went to Belgrade. For days the poverty-stricken student slept in the parks and went without food, while he dreamed of leading his people to freedom. On a trip back to Sarajevo in 1913 he joined the *Narodna Odbrana* (National Defense), a secret patriotic and terrorist society.

Below is the inside story of what has been called the most important murder in history. Borijove Jevtic, one of the leaders of *Narodna Odbrana,* was arrested immediately after the assassination. No evidence was obtained against him, and he was released after having been held in a cell next to that occupied by Princip. His first-hand description of the crime, substantiated by diplomatic documents on the assassination and by subsequent investigations, was published in *The New York World* on June 29, 1924.

A tiny clipping from a newspaper mailed without comment from a secret band of terrorists in Zagreb, capital of Croatia, to their comrades in Belgrade, was the torch which set the world afire with war in 1914. That bit of paper wrecked old, proud empires. It gave birth to new, free nations.

I was one of the members of the terrorist band in Belgrade which received it.

The little clipping declared that the Austrian Archduke Francis Ferdinand would visit Sarajevo, the capital of Bosnia, June 28, to direct army maneuvers in the neighboring mountains.

It reached our meeting place, the cafe called Zeatna Moruna, one night the latter part of April, 1914. To understand how great a sensation that little piece of paper caused among us when it was passed from hand to hand almost in silence, and how greatly it inflamed our hearts, it is necessary to explain just why the *Narodna Odbrana* existed, the kind of men that were in it, and the significance of that date, June 28, on which the Archduke dared to enter Sarajevo.

As every one knows, the old Austro-Hungarian Empire was built by conquest and intrigues, by sales and treacheries, which held in subjugation many peoples who were neither Austrian nor Hungarian. It taxed them heavily; it diverted the products of their toil to serve the wealth of the master state. It interfered in their old freedom by a multiplicity of laws administered with arrogance.

Several years before the war, a little group of us, thirty-five in all, living in several Bosnian and Herzegovinian cities and villages, formed the *Narodna Odbrana*, the secret society, the aim of which was to work for freedom from Austria and a union with Serbia. So strict was the police vigilance in Bosnia and Herzegovina that we set up our headquarters in Belgrade, the capital of our mother country.

The men who were terrorists in 1914 embraced all classes. Most of them were students. Youth is the time for the philosophy of action. There were also teachers, tradesmen and peasants, artisans and even men of the upper classes were ardent patriots. They were dissimilar in everything except hatred of the oppressor.

Such were the men into whose hands the tiny bit of newsprint was sent by friends in Bosnia that April night in Belgrade. At a small table in a very humble cafe, beneath a flickering gas jet we sat and read it. There was no advice nor admonition sent with it. Only four letters and two numerals were sufficient to make us unanimous, without discussion, as to what we should do about it. They were contained in the fateful date, June 28.

How dared Francis Ferdinand, not only the representative of the oppressor but in his own person an arrogant tyrant, enter Sarajevo on that day? Such an entry was a studied insult.

June 28 is a date engraved deep in the heart of every Serb, so that the day has a name of its own. It is called the *Vidovnan*. It is the day on which the old Serbian kingdom was conquered by the Turks at the battle of Amselfelde in 1389. It is also the day on which in the second Balkan War the Serbian armies took glorious revenge on the Turk for his old victory and for the years of enslavement. . .

As we read that clipping in Belgrade we knew what we would do to Francis

Ferdinand. We would kill him to show Austria there yet lived within its borders defiance of its rule. We would kill him to bring once more to the boiling point the fighting spirit of the revolutionaries and pave the way for revolt.

Our decision was taken almost immediately. Death to the tyrant!

Then came the matter of arranging it. To make his death certain twenty-two members of the organization were selected to carry out the sentence. At first we thought we would choose the men by lot. But here Gavrilo Princip intervened. . . . From the moment Ferdinand's death was decided upon he took an active leadership in its planning. Upon his advice we left the deed to members of our band, who were in and around Sarajevo, under his direction and that of Gabrinovic, a linotype operator on a Serbian newspaper. Both were regarded as capable of anything in the cause.

Then came the matter of getting them arms. Present at our meeting was Major Tankosic, leader of a band of Serbian *comittachi*, one of those bands of nationalist bandits who prey only on their country's enemies, who raid in Macedonia and other alien soil. He arranged that we should get from his band the necessary hand grenades and Browning automatic pistols.

These arms were sent through certain secret channels, which were always open to us in Bosnia, and found their way to a little town on the outskirts of Sarajevo. They remained there until two days before the assassination, when they were brought into Sarajevo, one by one, by the most innocent looking carriers, to the house of the school teacher Ilic. The night before the murder he took them to a bakeshop in the center of the town, where they were distributed next morning.

The fateful morning dawned. Two hours before Francis Ferdinand arrived in Sarajevo all the twenty-two conspirators were in their allotted positions, armed and ready. They were distributed 500 yards apart over the route along which the Archduke must travel from the railroad station to the Town Hall.

When Francis Ferdinand and his retinue drove from the station they were allowed to pass the first two conspirators. The motor cars were driving too fast to make an attempt feasible and in the crowd were many Serbians; throwing a grenade would have killed many innocent people.

When the car passed Gabrinovic, the compositor, he threw his grenade. It hit the side of the car, but Francis Ferdinand with presence of mind threw himself back and was uninjured. Several officers riding in his attendance were injured.

The cars sped to the Town Hall and the rest of the conspirators did not interfere with them. After the reception in the Town Hall General Potiorek the Austrian Commander, pleaded with Francis Ferdinand to leave the city, as it was seething with rebellion. The Archduke was persuaded to drive the shortest way out of the city and to go quickly.

The road to the maneuvers was shaped like the letter V, making a sharp turn at the bridge over the River Nilgacka. Francis Ferdinand's car could go fast enough until it reached this spot but here it was forced to slow down for the turn. Here Princip had taken his stand.

As the car came abreast he stepped forward from the curb, drew his automatic pistol from his coat and fired two shots. The first struck the wife of the Archduke, the Archduchess Sofia, in the abdomen. She was an expectant mother. She died instantly. The second bullet struck the Archduke close to the heart.

He uttered only one word, "Sofia" – a call to his stricken wife. Then his head fell back and he collapsed. He died almost instantly.

The officers seized Princip. They beat him over the head with the flat of their swords. They knocked him down, they kicked him, scraped the skin from his neck with the edges of their swords, tortured him, all but killed him.

The next day they put chains on Princip's feet, which he wore till his death. . . .

I was placed in the cell next to Princip's, and when Princip was taken out to walk in the prison yard I was taken along as his companion.

By October 12, the date of Princip's trial, his prison sufferings had worn him to a skeleton.

His sentence was twenty years imprisonment at hard labor, the death sentence being inapplicable because he was a minor.

Awakened in the middle of the night and told that he was to be carried off to another prison, Princip made an appeal to the prison governor.

"There is no need to carry me to another prison. My life is already ebbing away. I suggest that you nail me to a cross and burn me alive. My flaming body will be a torch to light my people on their path to freedom."

Europe was overwhelmed in the cascading events after the assassination. Austria-Hungary, through Foreign Minister Count Leopold von Berchtold, seized the opportunity to reassert her supremacy in the Balkans by dispatching, on July 23, 1914, an ultimatum demanding, among other things, that Serbia submit to Austrian domination in her police and law courts. William II had already pledged that he would support Austria in whatever demands she made (the so-called "blank check"). The Serbs submitted a conciliatory reply within the forty-eight hours allowed them, accepting most of the demands but rejecting the one calling for collaboration of Austrian officials, which menaced their sovereignty. The Serbs also offered to submit the entire matter to the Hague Permanent Court of Arbitration. But simultaneously they began mobilization.

All efforts to localize the conflict were futile. When Austria began mobilization, the Russians threatened a similar step the moment Serbia was invaded. In the fatalistic climate of 1914, mobilization meant war. Germany inquired what England would do if war were to begin; Sir Edward Grey, the British foreign minister, replied that England would do that which best served her interests. The oracle at Delphi could not have delivered a more dangerously ambiguous response. Grey further proposed a European conference to settle the crisis, but Germany declined on the ground that the quarrel could be localized.

Refusing to accept the Serbian reply, Austria declared war on July 28, 1914. Russia mobilized the next day. On August 1 Germany declared war on Russia, after demanding in vain that the Russians disarm. Germany declared war on France on August 3. All these important events took place one after the other in what seemed to be the fateful scenes of a Greek tragedy.

On the evening of August 3, with Great Britain on the verge of war, Edward Grey stood at the window of the Foreign Office in London, watching the lamp being lit at dusk. His words were gloomy: "The lamps are going out all over Europe; we shall not see them lit again in our lifetime."

Meanwhile, on August 2, 1914, the German ambassador at Brussels, Herr von Below Saleske, delivered a note to M. Davignon, Belgian minister for foreign affairs, asking for free transit. Germans promised to respect Belgian territory, to evacuate it on conclusion of peace, and to pay an indemnity for any damage caused by German troops. The Belgians refused. The German military machine then clanked across the border into Belgium.

On August 4, 1914, shortly after invasion, Theobald von Bethmann-Hollweg, the German imperial chancellor, appeared before the *Reichstag* to define Germany's position in the war. He admitted the violation of Belgian neutrality but promised that the injustice would be remedied as soon as the necessary military goal was attained. The neutrality of Belgium had been guaranteed in 1839 by the European powers; its violation brought England into the war. Italy, claiming that she was not bound under the terms of the Triple Alliance to assist in an offensive war, declared her neutrality.

In this tragic way the nations of Europe fell over the abyss. Since 1914, historians have busied themselves with the problem of placing responsibility for the war. Was the conflict the outcome of the general conditions of the day? Was it a clear-cut case of German aggression prepared for four decades? Was it the result of Britain going all the way to protect its empire against a fast-moving Germany? How much of it was due to Russia's belligerence and her Pan-Slavic policy?

And what about individual responsibility? How much blame should be placed on the blustering Austrian Berchtold, the loud-mouthed Emperor William II, the double-talking Edward Grey, or the indifferent Nicholas II? In the long run, could any individual have had strength enough to contain the flood?

Scholars pour over the documents — as if the printed word of official publications contains the truth. In the decades since 1914 the majority of historians have come to the conclusion that no one nation, not even Germany, should bear the brunt of responsibility for the outbreak of the war. They accept Lloyd George's judgment that the nations of Europe, all balanced precariously, fell over the precipice without actually wanting war. The cause, they say, lay in the temper of the times. Sarajevo was but the spark which set the fire to flammable material.

The academic battle refuses to remain stilled. Only recently Professor Fritz Fischer of the University of Hamburg published a study, *Germany's Aims in the First World War* (London, 1967), again based on the archives, accenting blame on Germany for the prewar crisis. The book, not exactly pleasing to Fischer's countrymen, added heat to the controversy. Experts may differ on the matter of responsibility, but one fact remains unchallenged — Europe and the world would never be the same after this major turning point of history.

SINKING OF THE *LUSITANIA*, MAY 7, 1915

"There was a low, weeping, wailing, inarticulate
sound, mingled with coughing and gargling."

On August 4, 1914, the German army, like a giant mechanical green monster, crossed the border and swept through the defenses of neutral Belgium. In line with the von Schlieffen Plan, the fast-moving army was supposed to swing in a wide arc and with its hammerhead hit Paris a knockout blow. The Germans would then transfer the bulk of their forces to the eastern front to smash the Russians. Like Bismarck's first two wars for national unification, this war was supposed to be finished within a few weeks.

Then came the unexpected first turning point. The defenders, helped by troops sent in taxicabs hurriedly from Paris, struck back in the First Battle of the Marne, September 6–12, and stopped the Germans in their tracks. The opposing armies settled down in trench warfare, in which millions of men dug themselves like moles into the ground and faced each other over a span of no man's land. This meant an end to the German dream of lightning victory. It was pure slaughter as angry, cootie-ridden men poured out their blood in vain attempts to gain a few yards of soil.

That stalemate was to be ended when the United States entered the war. In August 1914 American public opinion leaned in the direction of Germany and the Central Powers. The large German-American population sympathized with the *Vaterland*. Irish-Americans were anti-British. American Jews had little use for Czarist Russia and its pogroms.

The story of how Germany dissipated these assets from 1914 to 1917 is a classic case in the shifting of public opinion. Several German actions led to strong criticism in the United States. Americans were angered by the execution of Nurse Edith

Cavell on October 12, 1915 for harboring refugees and helping 130 of them to escape ("Patriotism is not enough; I have no hatred or bitterness towards anyone.") Other Americans took an anti-German position after the decoding of the Zimmermann telegram – a coded message of January 19, 1917 from the German Foreign secretary Arthur Zimmermann to the German minister in Mexico, urging the conclusion of a German-Mexican alliance so that, if the United States entered the war against Germany, the Mexicans would cross the American frontier.

But an earlier event contributed even more to bringing American entrance into World War I – the sinking of the Cunard liner *Lusitania* on May 7, 1915. This was the second major turning point in World War I. With its manpower and productive capacity the United States tipped the scales in favor of Allied victory.

The *"Lucy"* was a magnificent ship, the queen of the Cunard Line, and the fastest vessel on the seas. In 1915 terms, she was a floating castle. The *Lusitania* and her sister ship, the *Mauretania,* were built of steel in 1907 by John Brown and Company, at Clydebank, Scotland, under British Admiralty survey. She was a four-stacker, rigged fore and aft, with eight decks, an overall length of 785 feet, a beam of 88 feet, and a depth of 60 feet 4½ inches. Aboard this monster were some 192 furnaces, six turbines, and several dozen boilers.

The statistics were even more impressive. In the hull of the great ship were 26,000 steel plates, a few of them weighing as much as five tons, and all were held rigidly in place by 4,000,000 rivets. The rudder weighed 65 tons, and the three anchors were 10 tons each. Some 170 doors connected the compartments of the ship; it was believed that she would be watertight in emergencies. There were 200 miles of wiring aboard, including thousands of side lights and incandescent lights.

No wonder this liner was the pride of the English passenger fleet. Other countries had their luxury liners, too but the *Lusitania* surpassed all of them. Everything about her – her lounges, theatres, restaurants – was designed for comfort and beauty. Proud Englishmen referred to her as "our Goliath of the seas." She was, indeed, the Queen of the Atlantic.

The *Lusitania* was launched in June 1906, and she made her maiden voyage across the Atlantic in September 1907. The next year she won the blue ribbon, crossing from Queenstown to New York, a distance of 2,780 nautical miles, in just four days and 15 hours.

The *Lusitania*, said her builders, was unsinkable. She had a series of walls dividing her into cross sections: if the hull were pierced at any point, only one or two sections at the most could be flooded. So said the designers. More, to get even greater protection, the builders fitted her with longitudinal as well as transverse bulkheads. The boiler rooms and engine rooms were set well apart.

If, by chance, any water should penetrate into the ship, it would be confined, said the designers, to certain cross sections. This was "battleship construction," originated by Navy experts. The *Lusitania* would remain buoyant in case of trouble – it was said.

There were sufficient lifeboats and lifesaving apparatus aboard. No one had forgotten the sinking of the *Titanic*, the White Star Liner which had hit an iceberg on April 15, 1912, and had lost 1,513 persons out of 2,224 on board. Investigating commissions on both sides of the Atlantic found that the *Titanic* did not have enough lifeboats and life belts on board. The *Lusitania* had plenty of them. In a total of 48 lifeboats, 22 were ordinary Class-A lifeboats, 11 on each side of the boat deck. The remaining 26 were collapsible, 18 of them stowed under the lifeboats, and 8 on each side of the ship abaft the lifeboats. Each was equipped with water, biscuits, and other necessities in case of danger. At least 2,600 people could be taken care of in the lifeboats, more than was required on the *Lusitania's* last voyage.

In addition, there were 2,325 life belts distributed throughout the ship on racks and in staterooms. There were the familiar cork rings as well as the new body belts. At least 125 belts were specially designed for children. There were signs in each cabin giving directions concerning location of the life belts and directions for donning them.

Could this magnificent ship, with her long list of safety precautions, possibly fall victim to a German U-boat?

On Saturday morning, May 1, 1915, precisely at 10:30 a.m. the *Lusitania* was pulled from her pier on the Hudson River by tugs and turned downstream toward Sandy Hook and the open sea. The boat deck was lined with passengers taking their final look at the New York skyline, the Statue of Liberty, Ellis Island, and Coney Island. The day was clear and the water was smooth as the ship headed into the Atlantic. Captain William Thomas Turner ordered a course on a circle toward Ireland.

The passengers quickly settled into the routine of a transatlantic crossing. But some were worried about rumors. Was it true that some of the more important passengers had been warned by German agents on the Cunard pier not to sail on the *Lusitania*? And had not some passengers received telegrams insisting that they stay home this time? One rumor had it that Alfred Gwynne Vanderbilt, the millionaire sportsman, had received a wire: "Have it on definite authority that the *Lusitania* is to be torpedoed. You had better cancel immediately." Another report held that a passenger received a one-word message: *"Morte"* (Death).

But few took the rumors seriously. There were only several cancellations and that was routine. Some scary passengers had transferred to the *New York,* an American liner flying a neutral flag. But most of those on board the British vessel felt that the Germans would never dare attack an unarmed, defenseless passenger vessel, no matter what flag it was flying.

There had been precautions in New York. Each passenger was required to get in line and personally claim his luggage. All packages, but not trunks and valises, were opened by inspectors. Clerks carefully examined all tickets.

There were just 1,257 passengers on that voyage — well below the capacity of the *Lusitania*. With the crew this made a total of 1,959 on board. There were 290 passengers in first class (saloon), 600 in second class (cabin), and 367 in third class.

Of these, more than 900 were British and Canadian, and the remainder divided among eighteen other nationalities, including 6 Greeks, 3 Dutchmen, 1 Swiss, 5 Swedes, 3 Belgians, 2 Mexicans, 72 Russians, 8 Frenchmen, 2 Italians, 1 Indian, 1 Dane, 1 Spaniard, 1 Norwegian, 15 Persians, 1 Hindu, 1 Argentine, and 197 Americans.

Everyone had full faith in Captain Turner. He held an Extra Master's Certificate and had served the Cunard line for thirty-two years, since 1903 as Commodore of its passenger fleet. His plan was to take the *Lusitania* across Liverpool Bar, twelve miles from the port. He could cross only at high tide, due at 6:53 on the morning of May 8. He would have to pass through Saint George's Channel in darkness and cross the bar without stopping. It would be difficult to approach Liverpool Bar on dead reckoning: he would have to move to the Irish coast just long enough to make a formal landfall. He had to decide whether to keep offshore at the same distance as when he passed Fastnet, or work in to shore and head in close to Coningbeg Light Vessel. He weighed each possibility, and then decided on the latter course. This was best, he felt, because it would help him avoid any submarines lurking in mid-channel ahead of him. The idea was to delay the action until precisely the right moment.

Not only did Captain Turner have the problem of navigating his ship safely to Liverpool, he also had to maintain a sharp lookout for submarines. The British Admiralty, issuing general and specific orders, had repeatedly warned him of the menace. Between midnight of May 6-7, and 10:00 a.m. on May 7, he received the same warning seven times.

As the giant Cunarder approached the Irish coast at 8:00 a.m. on May 7, she encountered an intermittent fog – or Scotch mist – called "banks" by seamen. Captain Turner reduced the speed of his ship from 18 to 15 knots. He was determined to run the last leg of his voyage before daylight the next morning.

Between 8:00 a.m. and 11:00 a.m. the *Lusitania* passed south of Fastnet Rock Lighthouse which was not yet in sight but which was from 18½ to 25 miles distant. Captain Turner held up the course of his ship slightly to bring her closer to land. By noon the fog disappeared, and the ship's speed was increased to 18 knots. A little after noon, land was sighted abaft the port beam.

On that morning young Captain Walther Schwieger of the German submarine *U-20* surfaced his boat about twelve miles off the Old Head of Kinsale, Ireland. He had left Emden a week ago in search of enemy ships, and was now preparing to return to base with his crew of 35 men and six officers. In the last 48 hours he had shelled a sailing ship and destroyed two British steamers. Thus far the voyage had been highly successful.

Then came an electric instant as an officer shouted – a large steamer was approaching ahead and to starboard. There were four funnels and two masts, he said. She was coming on at a right-angle course. The news sped through the crew – here was a valuable victim. There was murder in the air.

Call to battle stations! The U-boat was quickly submerged to a depth of 220 feet. Then came the big question for Captain Schwieger. Should he give passengers and crew of his coming victim a chance to take to the lifeboats? That was the demand of international law. But Schwieger thought of Captain Weddigen, a colleague who had recently given warning to a prospective victim and as a result had lost his submarine and his life. No — Schwieger would not surface his craft and allow it to be rammed by that tremendous ship. Full speed ahead!

Meanwhile Captain Turner sighted the Old Head of Kinsale and turned his course to S.87 mag. That was exactly what the U-boat skipper wanted — he could now approach for a torpedo shot. Forward — maximum speed! He would soon be at a spot directly ahead of his prey.

It was 1:50 p.m. when Captain Turner ordered a four point bearing on the Old Head of Kinsale, about 10 to 15 miles off: this would allow him to steer a course up to Conigbeg. The bearing would take 20 to 30 minutes. There had been two wireless messages from the Admiralty saying that there were submarines in the vicinity. Captain Turner was sure that he had evaded them.

The *U-20* was running at her maximum speed. The crewmen were at their posts, awaiting the moment of attack. On command, they sent a torpedo directly toward the target.

Captain Schwieger entered the details in his log:

3:10 P.M. [Middle European Time; 2:10 P.M. Greenwich Time]: Clean bow shot at a distance of 700 meters [approximately ½ mile] (G-torpedo, three meters [10 feet] depth adjustment); angle 90°, estimated speed 22 knots. Torpedo hits starboard side directly behind the bridge.

"She was cutting the water like a razor!" a passenger later testified.

Hurtling swiftly through the surface of the smooth sea, the torpedo left a white wake as it made for the starboard side of the *Lusitania.* Some of the passengers had just finished lunch and were admiring the emerald green of the Irish coastline off the port beam. Several anxious voyagers joined in the lookout for a submarine attack.

At impact there was a muffled sound, much like that of an arrow striking a canvas target, but magnified many times. Smoke and steam rose up from the superstructure of the huge ship. The *Lusitania* trembled for a moment, as if she could not understand what had happened to her. Nor did her passengers know. Then within 30 seconds came a second explosion toward the center of the ship. That second explosion was to become the mysterious core of the whole incident. Was it another torpedo — or cold water hitting the steam boilers?

The *Lusitania,* carried by her own momentum, plunged forward for a distance of two to three miles. But within a matter of minutes she began to settle along her whole water line. Her compartments, which were supposed to hold in just such an emergency, were soon flooded. Gradually, almost in slow motion, the stern of the great hulk rose into the air. Then she began to go down by the bow.

Now the explosions followed one another rapidly as water struck the boilers. It was an unearthly sound. The great machines in the bowels of the ship began to cut through the bulkheads as if they were butter.

Passengers surged to the port side, then began to slide toward starboard as the motion of the sinking ship carried them across the decks. The lifeboats fell into crazy formations, some hanging from their davits, others slithering into the sea. Screaming, frantic passengers were hurled into the water.

Then came the final plunge – just 18 minutes from the instant when the torpedo struck. Just as a duck dives, so did the *Lusitania* go under the surface. She seemed to divide the water smoothly like a huge knife cutting the sea. Down went hundreds of trapped passengers, crewmen, the entire cargo, and the first American sacks of mail ever lost at sea during wartime.

It was a chaotic scene. On the surface was a great mass of floating wreckage – planks, crates, deck chairs, life belts, paper, and rope. Struggling passengers thrashed in the water, either clinging to wreckage or to each other in desperate attempts to save their lives. In this maelstrom of waving arms, humans tried to remain afloat. "Help us God!" "Please save us!" Such were the agonizing cries of passengers about to die.

Soon, the shouts and cries weakened on all sides. "Finally," said survivor Dr. Daniel V. More, an American physician, "there was a low weeping, wailing, inarticulate sound, mingled with coughing and gargling. It made me sick." It was the familiar sound of a sea tragedy.

According to the Mersey investigation figures, not completely accurate, the passengers were made up of 688 adult males, 440 adult females, 51 male children, 39 female children, and 39 infants.

– Of the 688 adult males, 421 were lost and 267 were saved.
– Of the 440 adult females, 270 were lost and 170 were saved.
– Of the 51 male children, 33 were lost and 18 were saved.
– Of the 39 female children, 26 were lost and 13 were saved.
– Of the 39 infants, 35 were lost, and 4 were saved.

The crew numbered 702 – 677 men and 25 women.

– Of the male members of the crew, 397 were lost and 280 saved.
– Of the female members of the crew, 16 were lost and 9 saved.

A total of 1,198 persons perished on the *Lusitania*. Of the Americans on board, 128 were lost and 69 were saved.

News of the disaster hit London with the impact of a hurricane. At first people refused to believe it. On the Strand a newsboy shouted, *"Lusitania* torpedoed and sunk! Official!" He was stopped outside the Hotel Cecil by a police constable who told the lad that he would be arrested if he were crying out false news. The boy showed the policeman the official report of the disaster in the "Stop-Press Column," whereupon he was allowed to go ahead. In a few minutes he was surrounded by a clamoring crowd which bought all his newspapers. For once the English reputation for understatement failed. One after another, Englishmen denounced the Germans. The offices of the Cunard Company were besieged with relatives begging for news of the disaster.

There was a key question. Was the *Lusitania* a warship or a passenger vessel? There were angry quarrels. According to international law a warship could be attacked on sight. But the sinking of a passenger vessel, even in wartime, was a violation of the law of nations.

The Germans had their own version. The German Foreign Office claimed that the *Lusitania* was in fact a warship and therefore open to destruction without warning. Had she not been built with funds supplied by the British government at a low rate of interest? The whole world knew that the Cunard liner had emplacements ready for mounted guns, for at least twelve of them. This was no passenger ship, said the Germans.

From Berlin came additional arguments. Captain Turner was actually a Commander in the British Royal Navy Reserve and he was under secret orders to ram any submarine he came across in the Atlantic. All any objective person had to do was to look in *Jane's Fighting Ships*. the British register of warships, and there he would find a silhouette of the *Lusitania* with the designation "armed merchantman." Berlin editorialists insisted that when the *Lusitania* sailed from New York on her final voyage, she was armed with four guns. Passenger ship? Nonsense! This was a real warship.

From London came denials of all these charges as plainly false. The responses were made to each charge:

1. Not only Britain but all governments of the Great Powers used national funds to construct merchant-marine vessels.

2. Warship of the British Navy? False! The *Lusitania* was a reserve ship, even as all fast passenger liners, including German, were to be considered in this special category.

3. Certainly the *Lusitania* was listed in *Jane's Fighting Ships,* but as a normal reserve ship. The Germans ought to understand that!

4. Admittedly, the *Lusitania* was taken over by the Admiralty in the opening days of the war. However, she used so much coal that she was promptly returned to the Cunard Line. Besides, what was the difference? The Germans were doing the same thing with their own ships. Why single out the British?

5. Even if Captain Turner was a Commander of the British Navy Reserve, what was wrong with that? Did not the Germans themselves follow this policy? Furthermore, note that neither the officers nor the crew of the *Lusitania – of this passenger ship* – were regular Navy men.

6. Equipped with mounted guns? Nonsense – this existed only in the imagination of German newspapermen. This, said the British, was an excellent example of the way in which emotional editorialists resorted to plain falsehood to strike back at the British.

Furthermore, London denied heatedly that there were any munitions on board the *Lusitania.* An examination of the manifesto would prove that there were no explosives listed. Yes, of course, there was *ammunition* on board, but there is a vast difference between *munitions* and *ammunition.* The manifesto in American files listed 5,471 cases of cartridges, 1,271 cases of unloaded shrapnel shells, and 4,200 cases of Remington cartridges for small arms. These were stored some fifty yards away from where the torpedo struck.

The British argued that, under a ruling of the United States courts, this part of the *Lusitania*'s cargo did not come under the category of munitions forbidden by American authorities. What the Germans were doing was to confuse permissible cargo for destructive war materials. That was unreasonable, unfair, just what one had come to expect of the Germans. The fact remained, said the British, that the Germans had performed a barbarous act and were using every argument under the sun — legal or illegal — to justify what was actually a war crime.

To all these explanations the Germans reacted furiously. One thing was certain: that ship carried explosives designed to kill Germans, hence she was a fair target for U-boats. Any intelligent human being knew that the Cunard liner would have remained afloat for a long time had it not been for those explosives she had in her hold. Was not the liner supposed to be unsinkable? How was it that an unsinkable ship could go down in just eighteen minutes? Any fool could see that explosives on board were responsible — despite all the sophistic arguments coming from London. This was, said the Germans, merely British hypocrisy.

The question has never been resolved satisfactorily. Could the heat generated by just one torpedo ignite the powder in the cartridges? What caused the second explosion? Was it one or a series of bursting boilers hitting the water? Were there actually unlisted explosives aboard the giant ship? Or was there some other reason? The mystery is there and it remains there.

The arguments went on and on. Meanwhile, American public opinion began to turn against Germany and the Central Powers. Why had Berlin been so stupid as to believe that it could sink an unarmed passenger ship with many Americans aboard and not pay the price for it? German military and naval leaders must have taken leave of their senses.

The sinking of the *Lusitania* was one of the more important episodes that led to American entry into the war. When the United States Congress declared war, German women wept in the streets — they knew what that meant. Emperor William II, as usual whistling in the dark, announced that those Americans never would be able to transport enough troops across the Atlantic. The blustering Hohenzollern was dead wrong.

There were any number of major and minor turning points in the war — the First Battle of the Marne, the battles of Tannenberg and the Masurian Lakes, Verdun — but the sinking of the *Lusitania* by a trigger-happy U-boat captain was a mistake of incalculable consequences. This offense against American neutrality was the convincing act that brought a mighty newcomer into the war and sealed the fate of the Germans.

STORMING OF THE WINTER PALACE, NOVEMBER 7, 1917

"Comrades! Don't touch anything! Property of the people!"

MASS action does not in itself automatically mean a turning point in history. Usually the change occurs when a social movement receives direction from a group of dedicated leaders. Without effective leadership mob action descends into anarchic chaos with eventual punishment for the rebels and triumph of the *status quo*.

A classic example is the November 1917 Bolshevik Revolution in which a handful of determined men led the Russian masses in a rebellion against an earlier revolution and diverted the course of history into a channel of their own choosing. A bald little man, with sharp eyes and a goatee, gave direction to a ready-made historical turning point based on the teachings of Karl Marx.

At the outbreak of World War I in August 1914, Russia was allied with France and England against the Central Powers, Germany and Austria-Hungary. The Russian people rallied around their leaders, and even Czar Nicholas II began to enjoy a new popularity. At first the news was good — there were reports of great victories at the front. But then came the unvarnished truth of defeat. A giant Russian army was trapped at Tannenberg, August 26-30, 1914, and another was destroyed at the Masurian Lakes, September 6-15, 1914.

It became clear that the Russian army was not prepared for war. Military leaders were weak and some were dishonest. Drunken officers sent unarmed soldiers into battle. The men fought bravely until they realized that they had no chance of victory, whereupon they just dropped their weapons and went home. There were shortages of food, medicine, nearly everything. Land-hungry peasants and starving workers began to talk of revolution.

On March 8, 1917, there was a gala performance for the fur-clad nobility in the Alexander Theater in Petrograd. Outside in the bitter cold, long lines of women waited in front of the bakery shops. The next day more than a hundred thousand angry workers went on strike, joined by women demanding peace and bread for their children. To the Cossacks patrolling the streets with drawn swords the strikers shouted, "Don't attack us, brothers! All we want is bread."

"We know," answered the Cossacks. "We are hungry, too."

On March 10 there were large crowds milling in the streets. The troops fired their rifles, killing 200 people.

The Czar, who was at the battle front, had left the government in the hands of the Duma without power to act. Hurriedly, the ministers wired him: "Situation serious. Anarchy reigns. We must form a new government. Delay may be fatal."

A man of limited imagination, the Czar knew only one answer to this kind of problem. Again and again the Empress had told him, "Russia likes to feel the whip." Once again he ordered his troops to move against the people. This time the soldiers refused to use their guns. On the morning of March 12, angered soldiers shot the officers who had ordered them to fire. Whole regiments joined the mutiny. Together with the workers they broke into the arsenals, appropriated 40,000 rifles, and gave them to the people. Police and army officers fled the city.

By that night the revolution was over. More than a thousand people, both soldiers and civilians, were killed or wounded. Within a week the revolution spread throughout the empire. The Czar started for Petrograd by train, but his way was barred by striking railway workers. On March 15, two delegates from the Duma met him in his railway carriage and told him that he must relinquish his throne. Nicholas asked for a sheet of paper and drew up his abdication: "The Lord God has been pleased to send down on Russia a new and heavy trial. We have thought it well to renounce the throne of the Russian Empire and to lay down the supreme power. May the Lord God help Russia!"

The revolution took place, said Milyukov, one of its leaders, "because history does not know of another government so stupid, so dishonest, so cowardly, so treacherous as the government now overthrown." The provisional government, under the leadership of Prince Lvov, a liberal aristocrat, sought to carry on the war against Germany and at the same time to transform Russia into a modern democracy. This task was never accomplished.

The new government survived only seven months. The people, defeated, starved, exhausted, embittered, yearned for peace. Discipline at the front evaporated as thousands of troops deserted. Peasants seized the estates; workingmen occupied the factories. Into this chaotic situation stepped a small group of determined men who had studied the dynamics of popular control and who directed the vast, surging mood of indignation into the channels of a second revolution. This time the bourgeois state was overthrown in favor of a proletarian dictatorship.

The clue to victory was superbly effective leadership. Two men who came forward to lead the revolution — a fanatic who called himself Lenin, and an intellectual who called himself Trotsky.

Lenin's real name was Vladimir Ilyich Ulyanov. Like most Russian revolutionaries he had changed his name to avoid being caught by the police. He was born on April 9 (22), 1870, at Simbirsk, a small city on the Volga River. His father was an inspector of schools. The third of seven children in a religious, hard-working family, Lenin had a happy country childhood. When he was seventeen his older brother was hanged with four fellow students for trying to kill Czar Alexander III. To the day of his death Lenin was consumed with hatred for those responsible for his brother's death.

While he was a university student, Lenin read the works of Karl Marx. Inspired by the dream of a state run by the workers, he joined the Social Democratic party and began to work secretly to organize for revolution. In 1895 he was arrested by the police and imprisoned. Two years later he was exiled to Siberia. Released in 1900, he went to Munich, to join other Social Democrats who were working for world revolution. When the party split in 1903, he became leader of the Bolsheviks.

For Lenin revolution was a science to be studied as an engineer works out the problem of building a bridge. A revolutionary genius with a talent for getting things done, he was also completely ruthless. Listening to piano music by Beethoven in Moscow one evening, he said, "I know nothing which is greater than Beethoven's music. It is marvelous, superhuman." Then screwing up his eyes, he added, "But I can't listen to music very often. It makes you want to say stupid nice things. It makes you want to stroke the heads of people who can create such beauty while living in this vile hell. But you mustn't stroke anyone's head — you might get your hand bitten off. You have to hit them on the head, without mercy."

This hard, vigorous man guided the Bolshevik Revolution and founded the Soviet Union. To Communists he became a god. To his enemies he was the first of the twentieth-century dictators, a tyrant who let nobody and nothing stand in his way to absolute power.

Leon Trotsky, the second leading figure of the Bolshevik Revolution, was the son of a well-to-do farmer in the Russian steppe. His real name was Lev Davidovich Bronstein. Before he was twenty years old he was imprisoned as a radical but no prison seemed stronge enough to hold him.

While organizing cells, groups of revolutionists, Trotsky was caught and sent into exile in Siberia. There his wife rigged up a dummy in his bed and held off the police for four days by saying he was too ill to be disturbed. Meanwhile, he escaped and made his way back home with a false passport. When the police got on his trail again, he smuggled himself out of Russia in a peasant cart. A thinker and a dreamer, Trotsky was also a man of action.

Lenin was in Switzerland when the March Revolution erupted. The news that the workers had risen against the Czar convinced him that they were ready for the "true" revolution which would do away not only with the Czar but with the whole Russian upper class. Eager to return to Russia, he asked the Germans to send him across their territory by railroad to the borders of his country. The Germans were willing — Lenin was a useful troublemaker who would take Russia out of the war. But they took care to seal the train: to them he was, in the words of Winston Churchill, "like a plague bacillus."

Lenin arrived at the Finland Station in Petrograd on the evening of April 16,

1917 to find a great crowd waiting to greet him. Red banners were everywhere. A searchlight moved its beam across the faces of the crowd. Wearing a round cap and carrying a huge bouquet of flowers, Lenin stepped to the platform. His face looked frozen, according to an eyewitness. He stopped to make a short speech.

"Dear comrades," he said. "Soldiers, sailors and workers! I am happy to greet in you the victorious Russian Revolution. I greet you as the first of the worldwide workers' army. Any day now the whole of European capitalism may crash. The Russian Revolution accomplished by you has opened a new epoch. Long live the worldwide Socialist Revolution!"

Lenin found exactly the situation he expected and wanted. Workers were staying away from their jobs. The peasants were refusing to pay rent or taxes, the soldiers were unwilling to fight. Most Russians were exhausted and bitterly opposed to the new government. Lenin knew how to win the people. He used an attractive slogan, *"Peace! Land! Bread!"* and hammered away with these three words at the unhappy people. The soldiers and everybody else wanted peace, the workers wanted bread, and the peasants wanted land. The peasants little dreamed that "land" meant not plots for themselves but land controlled by the state.

With Trotsky's help, Lenin took over the leadership of the soviets, councils of workers, peasants, and soldiers. Then the two men began their final drive for power.

On November 5 the cruiser *Aurora* was anchored in the Neva River in Petrograd. Under orders from the soviets, the sailors landed and helped the Bolshevik Red Guards seize and lower the bridges over the river. The next night, November 6, a force of workers, soldiers, and sailors attacked the main railway station and captured the remaining bridges.

The morning of November 7 was raw and chilly. The street cars were still running, small boys hanging from the sides as usual. The Bolsheviks took over the State Bank and the main telephone building. The people in charge offered very little resistance. Kerensky, now the Provisional Prime Minister, escaped to the front to bring back loyal troops to crush the revolt.

By nightfall all that remained of the government was in the Winter Palace. Barricaded in this vast building were thirteen government ministers, about 1,000 yunkers (young military cadets), 130 members of the Women's Battalion of Death (a fighting unit), and a few loyal Cossacks. This was the moment for which Lenin had been waiting. He ordered an attack on the Winter Palace.

Life went on as usual in the city, though armored cars cruised the streets and searchlights played on the palace walls. Suddenly the assault came.

In his *Ten Days That Shook the World,* John Reed recorded in broad sweeping strokes the steps by which the Bolsheviks seized power. To Reed his own work was "a slice of intensified history — history as I saw it." To Lenin it was "a truthful and most vivid exposition." To Granville Hicks, Reed's biographer, it was "the drama of great events, clearly understood and objectively recounted. The poet in him made every detail vivid; the revolutionary made every detail significant." Following are excerpts from this remarkable book: [1]

Wednesday, November 7, I rose very late. The noon cannon boomed from Peter-Paul as I went down the Nevsky. It was a raw, chill day. In front of the State Bank some soldiers with fixed bayonets were standing at the closed gates.

"What side do you belong to?" I asked. "The government?"

"No more government," one answered with a grin, *"Slava Bogu!* Glory to God!" That was all I could get out of him.

The streetcars were running on the Nevsky, men, women, and small boys hanging on every projection. Shops were open, and there seemed even less uneasiness among the street crowds than there had been the day before. A whole crop of new appeals against insurrection had blossomed out on the walls during the night — to the peasants, to the soldiers at the front, to the workmen of Petrograd.

I bought a copy of *Rabotchi Put,* the only newspaper which seemed on sale, and a little later paid a soldier fifty kopecks for a secondhand copy of *Dien.* The Bolshevik paper, printed on large-sized sheets in the conquered office of the Russkaya Volia, had huge headlines: ALL POWER — TO THE SOVIETS OF WORKERS, SOLDIERS, AND PEASANTS! PEACE! BREAD! LAND!

Just at the corner of the Ekaterina Canal, under an arc light, a cordon of armed sailors was drawn across the Nevsky, blocking the way to a crowd of people in columns of fours. There were about three or four hundred of them, men in frock coats, well-dressed women, officers — all sorts and conditions of people.

Like a black river, filling all the streets, without song or cheer we poured through the Red Arch, where the man just ahead of me said in a loud voice: "Look out, comrades! Don't trust them. They will fire, surely!" In the open we began to run, stooping low and bunching together, and jammed up suddenly behind the pedestal of the Alexander Column.

After a few minutes' huddling there some hundreds of men, the army seemed reassured and without any orders suddenly began again to flow forward. By this time, in the light that streamed out of all the Winter Palace windows, I could see that the first two or three hundred men were Red Guards, with only a few scattered soldiers. Over the barricade of firewood we clambered, and leaping down inside gave a triumphant shout as we stumbled on a heap of rifles thrown down by the yunkers who had stood there. On both sides of the main gateway the doors stood wide open, light streamed out, and from the huge pile came not the slightest sound.

Carried along by the eager wave of men, we were swept into the right-hand entrance, opening into a great bare vaulted room, the cellar of the east wing, from which issued a maze of corridors and staircases. A number of huge packing cases stood about, and upon these the Red Guards and soldiers fell furiously, battering them open with the butts of their rifles, and pulling out carpets, curtains, linens, porcelain plates, glassware. One man went strutting around with a bronze clock perched on his shoulder; another found a plume of ostrich feathers, which he stuck in his hat. The looting was just beginning when

---

[1] From John Reed, *Ten Days That Shook the World* (New York, 1919), pp. 99 ff. Courtesy of Boni and Liveright.

somebody cried, "Comrades! Don't touch anything! Don't take anything! Property of the people!" Many hands dragged the spoilers down. Damask and tapestry were snatched from the arms of those who had them; two men took away the bronze clock. Roughly and hastily the things were crammed back in their cases, and self-appointed sentinels stood guard. It was all utterly spontaneous. Through corridors and up staircases the cry could be heard growing fainter and fainter in the distance, "Revolutionary discipline! Property of the people."

We crossed back over to the left entrance, in the west wing. There order was also being established. "Clear the palace!" bawled a Red Guard, sticking his head through an inner door. "Come, comrades, let's show that we're not thieves and bandits. Everybody out of the palace except the Commissars, until we get sentries posted."

Two Red Guards, a soldier and an officer, stood with revolvers in their hands. Another soldier sat at a table behind them, with pen and paper. Shouts of "All out! All out!" were heard far and near within, and the army began to pour through the door, jostling, expostulating, arguing. As each man appeared he was seized by the self-appointed committee, who went through his pockets and looked under his coat. Everything that was plainly not his property was taken away, the man at the table noted it on his paper, and it was carried into a little room. The most amazing assortment of objects were thus confiscated; statuettes, bottles of ink, bedspreads worked with the imperial monogram, candles, a small oil painting, desk blotters, gold-handled swords, cakes of soap, clothes of every description, blankets. One Red Guard carried three rifles, two of which he had taken away from yunkers; another had four portfolios bulging with written documents. The culprits either sullenly surrendered or pleaded like children. All talking at once, the committee explained that stealing was not worthy of the people's champions; often those who were caught turned around and began to help go through the rest of the comrades.

We asked if we might go inside. The committee was doubtful, but the big Red Guard answered firmly that it was forbidden. "Who are you anyway?" he asked. "How do I know that you are not all Kerenskys?" (There were five of us, two women.)

In the meanwhile unrebuked we walked into the palace. There was still a great deal of coming and going, of exploring newfound apartments in the vast edifice, of searching for hidden garrisons of yunkers which did not exist. We went upstairs and wandered through room after room. This part of the palace had been entered also by other detachments from the side of the Neva. The paintings, statues, tapestries, and rugs of the great state apartments were unharmed; in the offices, however, every desk and cabinet had been ransacked, the papers scattered over the floor, and in the living rooms beds had been stripped of their coverings and wardrobes wrenched open. The most highly prized loot was clothing, which the working people needed. In a room where furniture was stored we came upon two soldiers ripping the elaborate Spanish leather upholstery from chairs. They explained it was to make boots with.

The old palace servants in their blue and red and gold uniforms stood nervously about, from force of habit repeating, "You can't go in there, *barin!* It is forbidden —"

All this time, it must be remembered, although the Winter Palace was surrounded, the government was in constant communication with the front and with provincial Russia. The Bolsheviki had captured the Ministry of War early in the morning, but they did not know of the military telegraph office in the attic, nor of the private telephone line connecting it with the Winter Palace. In that attic a young officer sat all day, pouring out over the country a flood of appeals and proclamations; and when he heard that the palace had fallen, put on his hat and walked calmly out of the building.

Interested as we were, for a considerable time we didn't notice a change in the attitude of the soldiers and Red Guards around us. As we strolled from room to room a small group followed us, until by the time we reached the great picture gallery where we had spent the afternoon with the yunkers, about a hundred men surged in after us. One giant of a soldier stood in our path, his face dark with sullen suspicion.

"Who are you?" he growled. "What are you doing here?" The others massed slowly around, staring and beginning to mutter.

"Provocatori!" I heard somebody say. "Looters!" I produced our passes from the Military Revolutionary Committee. The soldier took them gingerly, turned them upside down, and looked at them without comprehension. Evidently he could not read. He handed them back and spat on the floor. *"Bumagi!* Papers!"* said he with contempt. The mass slowly began to close in, like wild cattle around a cowpuncher on foot. Over their heads I caught sight of an officer, looking helpless, and shouted to him. He made for us, shouldering his way through.

"I'm the Commissar," he said to me. "Who are you? What is it?" The others held back, waiting. I produced the papers.

"You are foreigners?" he rapidly asked in French. "It is very dangerous." Then he turned to the mob, holding up our documents. "Comrades!" he cried. "These people are foreign comrades — from America. They have come here to be able to tell countrymen about the bravery and the revolutionary discipline of the proletarian army!"

"How do you know that?" replied the big soldier. "I tell you they are provocators! They say they have come here to observe the revolutionary discipline of the proletarian army, but they have been wandering freely through the palace, and how do we know they haven't got their pockets full of loot?"

"Pravilno!" snarled the others, pressing forward.

"Comrades! Comrades!" appealed the officer, sweat standing out on his forehead. "I am Commissar of the Military Revolutionary Committee. Do you trust me? Well, I tell you that these passes are signed with the same names that are signed to my pass!"

He led us down through the palace and out through a door opening onto the Neva quay, before which stood the usual committee going through pockets. "You have narrowly escaped," he kept muttering, wiping his face.

We came out into the cold, nervous night, murmurous with obscure armies on the move, electric with patrols. From across the river, where loomed the darker mass of Peter-Paul, came a hoarse shout. Underfoot the sidewalk was littered with broken stucco, from the cornice of the palace where two shells from the battleship *Aurora* had struck; that was the only damage done by the bombardment.

It was now about three in the morning. On the Nevsky all the street lights were again shining, the cannon gone, and the only signs of war were Red Guards and soldiers squatting around fires. The city was quiet — probably never so quiet in its history; on that night not a single holdup occurred, not a single robbery.

The last act of the Bolshevik Revolution was over in two hours. This time there was little bloodshed. Only one soldier and five sailors were killed in the storming of the Winter Palace.

All throughout Russia there were similar scenes as the Red Guards took over local governments. All power was taken by the soviets, who set up a Council of People's Commissars, or heads of government departments. Lenin was President, Trotsky was Commissar of Foreign Affairs. Joseph Stalin, one day to be dictator of Soviet Russia, was given a minor post.

This was the great social experiment of the twentieth century, an attempt to invert the pyramidal structure of Russian society bottom side up. It was a revolution within a revolution, truly a major turning point in the historical current of modern times.

BATTLE OF BRITAIN, 1940

"This was their finest hour."

"MAY God Help the German people if ever a Napoleon appears among them!"

Thus spoke Johann Wolfgang von Goethe, Germany's greatest literary light and a keen observer of the ways of his countrymen. Germany did get her Napoleon, even worse, in the person of an Austrian hillbilly, a nasty, brutish little man with a Charlie Chaplin mustache and an ego as lofty as a Bavarian mountain. Adolf Hitler rose to become the dictator of Germany and master of Europe, and in the process dragged down the name of Germany into the mud of barbarism. Seldom since the days of Attila has the world seen so evil a leader.

In the opening year of World War II Hitler bestrode the continent like a giant colossus. His war machine had defeated Norway and smashed Holland and Belgium. He humbled France in an extraordinary *Blitzkrieg* and entered Paris as conqueror.

But all was not perfect for the Nazi *Fuehrer*. Once again as in the Napoleonic era the shadow of Britain stood in the way of final conquest. How that island resisted Hitler forms another great turning point in history. It was the age-old story — it is extraordinarily difficult to defeat a people who refuse to be beaten.

In the critical days after the fall of France, British leaders were most concerned about what would happen to the French fleet. They were not impressed by Hitler's promise not to use the French navy, nor did anyone of normal intelligence place any trust in the *Fuehrer's* word.

There was a saving factor — most of the French fleet was stationed in Oran in French North Africa. On July 3, 1940, three British warships moved into the port. The commander of the British force sent in an ultimatum. Either the French would join with the British — they could move into British ports, where their ships would be interned, or they could go to the West Indies and remain there until the end of the war. The decision was to be made within six hours or the French fleet would be destroyed.

Rejecting the ultimatum, the French decided to fight. With extreme reluctance, the British opened fire. Their guns disabled three French battleships, a seaplane carrier, and several lesser vessels.

While this drama was being played out, there came from inside Germany these challenging words from Hitler: "I am not the vanquished seeking favors, but the victor speaking in the name of reason." He called for "a common-sense peace through negotiations." He wanted the world to see him as a kindly man who was inclined to be magnanimous. All he wanted was recognition of his conquests, the return of Germany's colonies, and acceptance of his role as the arbiter of European affairs. Above all, he said, Winston Churchill had to be thrown out of office. "It was, perhaps," said British historian J. W. Wheeler-Bennett, "the most outstanding example of the 'love-hate' complex toward Britain which so many Germans through the ages have shared with Wilhelm II and Adolf Hitler."

Perhaps it might indeed have been wise for the British to accept Hitler's offer. They were obviously in a precarious position. One by one their allies had fallen victim to the Nazi chieftain. Their expeditionary force in Norway had been driven from the country and their troops on the continent had been thrown into the sea.

To the demanding *Fuehrer* the Britons replied with a contemptuous silence. Nothing, however, could stop the voice of Winston Churchill:

> Upon this battle depends the survival of Christian civilization. Upon it depends our British life, and the long continuity of our institutions and our Empire. The whole fury and might of the enemy must very soon be turned on us. Hitler knows that he will have to break us in this island or lose the war. If we can stand up to him, all Europe may be free and the life of the world may move forward into broad, sunlit uplands. But if we fail, then the whole world, including the United States, including all that we have known and cared for, will sink into the abyss of a new Dark Age. . . .
>
> Let us brace ourselves to our duties and so bear ourselves that, if the British Empire and its Commonwealth last for a thousand years, men will still say, "This was their finest hour."

Those were golden words from a master statesman. Under the impact of such phrases, all Englishmen, from aristocrat to fishmonger, from lady to servant girl, rallied to the cause. It was plainly and simply an unbeatable spirit.

Thus far the Germans had not made ready for a cross-Channel move. Hitler had hesitated at Dunkirk, probably because he had feared an attack from the rear by the French. He was playing it by ear, or to mix the metaphor by *Fingerspitzenge-fühl* ("fingertip feeling"). Whatever part of the anatomy he used, he still did not understand the quality of his British foe.

Meanwhile, the islanders went about the business of transforming their country into a mighty fortress. Nothing was allowed to stay in the way of defense. Spies and fifth-columnists were quickly rounded up and removed from circulation. Elderly men volunteered for civil defense and for essential services. Factories hummed on a round-the-clock schedule. Trenches were dug in the cities, and concrete pillars were placed at strategic spots in the open fields to discourage enemy planes. Target areas were covered with an umbrella of balloons flown on steel cables. Obviously, these embattled Britishers were counting on a fight to the finish. Adolf Hitler would be bewildered and frustrated by this kind of behavior.

What could the British do against the overwhelming force threatening them? Their defense seemed to be weak. In the Royal Air Force there were only 1,475 first-line planes which could be used against 2,670 German aircraft ordered to move against England. True, radar had been perfected, and this turned out to be a vital and decisive weapon in the coming months.

The order for attack came from Hermann Goering on August 8, 1940. Swarms of German planes appeared over the coastal towns of southern England, landing fields, and aircraft factories. This was to be another exercise in German efficiency — the British would be deprived of their air power in sudden, perfectly planned assaults.

So it seemed to the confident Germans, but the men who flew the planes were destined for a rude shock. Rising in Spitfires and Hurricanes to meet them were fighters of the R.A.F. — Englishmen, Poles, Czechs, Frenchmen, and Belgians. The aerial scene turned into a wild jamboree of twisting, tangling, flame-spitting planes, moving in a crazy din of machine-gun fire. Goering's airmen tried desperately to break their way through to their targets. Some crashed in plumes of smoke, while others rocketed into the Channel.

On the first day of this incredible battle, more than fifty Nazi fliers met a flaming death. The score mounted day by day as the Germans returned. In one August week alone, the *Luftwaffe* lost 256 planes.

It was unmitigated failure. The *Fuehrer* had not been able to drive his enemy from the skies. Churchill paid a magnificent tribute:

> The gratitude of every home in our Island, in our Empire, and indeed throughout the world, except in the abodes of the guilty, goes out to the British airmen who, undaunted by odds, unwearied in their constant challenge and mortal danger, are turning the tide of the World War by their prowess and by their devotion. Never in the field of human conflict was so much owed by so many to so few.

An angered *Fuehrer* decided to strike terror into the hearts of this enemy by hitting London as he had smashed Warsaw and Rotterdam. Attacks on the British capital had already been made. German airmen were sure that they could wipe the city from the face of the earth. Witness these words, dated August 18, 1940, from the diary of a German aviator, Gottfried Leske, in *I Was a Nazi Flier* (1941):

"Today I flew over the biggest city in the world. I knew with absolute certainty, as though I could foretell the future: This all will be destroyed. It will stand but a few days more. Until the moment the *Fuehrer* pronounces its death sentence. Then there will be nothing left but a heap of ruins."

Hitler stepped up the fury of the attack. His first mass onslaught on London came on September 7, 1940, when huge flights of German planes attacked. "This is the historic hour," said Goering, "when our air force for the first time delivered its stroke right into the enemy's heart."

T. H. O'Brien, a British historian, summarized the results of *Luftwaffe* operations against London on September 7 and 8, 1940:

> Between five and six o'clock on the evening of Saturday, 7 September, some 320 German bombers supported by over 600 fighters flew up the Thames and proceeded to bomb Woolwich Arsenal, Beckton Gas Works, a large number of docks, West Ham power station, and then the City, Westminster and Kensington. They succeeded in causing a serious fire situation in the docks. An area of about 1½ square miles between North Woolwich Road and the Thames was almost destroyed, and the population of Silvertown was surrounded by fire and had to be evacuated by water.
>
> At 8:10 p.m. some 250 bombers resumed the attack, which was maintained until 4:30 on Sunday morning. They caused 9 conflagrations, 59 large fires and nearly 1,000 lesser fires. Three main-line railway termini were put out of action, and 430 persons killed and some 1,600 seriously injured.
>
> After the fire brigade had spent all day in an effort to deprive the enemy of illumination, some 200 bombers returned at 7:30 in the evening to carry on the assault. During this second night a further 412 persons were killed and 747 seriously injured, and damage included the temporary stoppage of every railway line to the south.

Churchill issued a defiant judgment on Hitler: "This wicked man... this monstrous product of former wrongs and shame, has now resolved to try to break our famous Island race by a process of indiscriminate slaughter and destruction."

During the next three weeks the planes of the *Luftwaffe* roared in from Calais and up the Thames valley to the great metropolis. They flew over in mass formations of 250 craft, sometimes in small flights of a dozen planes, dropping tons of explosives and incendiaries and hitting docks, churches, factories, and railways.

On September 13, 1940, bombs hit near Buckingham Palace, destroying many windows in the Royal residence and leaving huge craters in the courtyard. Several days later the Germans made a mass daylight attack on targets in southern England.

Londoners were stunned but they refused to think of surrender. American reporters stationed in London were unanimous in their praise of the behavior of Englishmen in this crisis. They described the calm attitude of the average individual as amazing. They told how commuting suburbanites placidly bragged to fellow passengers on the morning trains about the size of the bomb craters in their neighborhoods, just as in more peaceful times they would have discussed their rose bushes. It was a nightmare, but the people reacted with courage, good humor, and kindliness.

Truly this was an almost unique display of patience and fortitude under dangerous conditions. Londoners were modest about their reaction. One smiling citizen said: "Don't call us heroes! It is just that we British lack imagination!" There were some minor complaints but they were uttered with true British understatement. A retired army officer sent a letter to a journal in which he said plaintively that too many war bulletins were bad for the nerves. "Let us have instead lectures on our historical and gallant fights for freedom and also a few calming nature talks."

The Britons worried about the effect of bombing noise on the country's bird population. The London press reported gravely that Monkey Hill at the Zoo had received a direct hit, "but the morale of the monkeys remained unaffected." Despite the food shortage, Englishmen made special efforts to keep their pets alive.

On October 1, 1940, Edward R. Murrow reported over the Columbia Broadcasting System:

> Today, in one of the most famous streets of London, I saw soldiers at work clearing away the wreckage of nearly an entire block. The men were covered with white dust. Some of them wore goggles to protect their eyes. They thought maybe people were still buried in the basements. The sirens sounded, and still they tore at the beams and bricks covering the place where the basements used to be.
>
> They are still working tonight. I saw them after tonight's raid started. They paid no attention to the burst of antiaircraft fire overhead as they bent their backs and carried away basketfuls of mortar and brick. A few small steam shovels would help them considerably in digging through those ruins. But all the modern instruments seem to be overhead. Down here on the ground people must work with their hands.

In a final desperate effort to cow this persistent enemy, the Germans unveiled a delayed-action bomb, which the British promptly dubbed the UXB, or unexploded bomb. The projectile buried itself into the ground and exploded later. For the Civil Defense Services there was no way to ascertain whether the buried projectile was a UXB or an ordinary bomb that had failed to explode. On September 12, 1940, a huge UXB, weighing at least a ton, fell into the outer foundations of St. Paul's Cathedral. A bomb-disposal squad removed the bomb while a gas main burned nearby.

Perplexed by British toughness and made hesitant by heavy plane losses, Hitler in October 1940 ordered a shift from daylight to night bombing. He would give the enemy no sleep and at the same time reduce his own losses by shifting the target area from London to the Midland industrial cities. By the end of October the pace of attack began to slow down.

The Germans were not yet ready to call it quits. They continued the air onslaught until June 1941. Most of the *Luftwaffe* was shifted to the Russian front, where it was desperately needed. One special Nazi attack aroused the interest of the entire world. On the night of November 14–15, 1940, German bombers struck at Coventry in the Midlands. The famed fourteenth-century cathedral, except for its 303-foot spire, was left a tangle of rubble.

Six weeks later London was the victim of a savage incendiary raid. More than a thousand fires were started in the heart of the City, including such old landmarks as the Guildhall and eight Wren churches. A remarkable defense and some good luck saved St. Paul's from destruction in this raid.

The next spring Goering shifted his main attack from London to the towns of Hull, Plymouth, and Bristol. At the same time he continued strikes at Manchester, Liverpool, and Birmingham.

The British paid a heavy toll. Nearly 13,000 Londoners lost their lives in the first three months of the raids. During the war the Germans dropped what has been estimated as 12,222 tons of bombs on London alone. Official British records show that 29,890 were killed and more than 120,000 injured as a result of German bombing. Many lives were lost and there had been tremendous material damage, but the fact remains that Goering's *Luftwaffe* was never able to stop British production or halt the flow of shipping.

From July 10 to October 31, 1940, the Germans lost (according to their own records) 1,733 aircraft in the attempt to humble Britain. Churchill reported that in this time 915 fighters were lost by the Royal Air Force (complete write-off or missing).

The Germans came out second best in the struggle because of a combination of circumstances. First, they were overconfident in a situation that obviously called for careful planning and action. Moreover, by shifting from target to target, Hitler made the error of striking with a maximum force at too many scattered points. The chances were that he might have been more successful had he concentrated on one target at a time. He was determined to break the British spirit — a task in which he was completely unsuccessful.

That British spirit was one of the wonders of the twentieth century. Accustomed to people knuckling down before his oratory and dive bombers, Hitler was perplexed to find a nation that stood up and struck back. In December 1940 a motion was made in the House of Commons to consider peace. It was voted down, 341-4. Such was language the monomaniac of Berchtesgaden could understand.

Hitler's war machine until this time had seemed to be unbeatable. Every time the German *Blitzkrieg* went into action it pulverized all opposition in its path. Even the French army, supposed to be among the strongest in the world and protected by its vaunted Maginot Line, was smashed quickly. But the seemingly irresistible Nazi flood changed its course when it hit the rock of British resistance.

This, then, was the initial turning point in the fortunes of the Austrian demagogue, his Nazi party, and Germany. Hitler knew well that occupation of the entire

European continent meant little unless he could destroy British power on its flank. He failed in this critical task.

In the cruel business of war it often matters little who wins the early stages of combat. Most armed aggressors are quite able to achieve quick victories by taking advantage of ill-prepared adversaries. The important thing is to win the final battle. Germany's raucous Napoleon was beaten finally by a combination of British resolve, Russian intransigence, and American power.

EPIC OF STALINGRAD, 1942

"Stay and fight! I am not leaving the Volga!"

MANY battles are surrounded with the aura of legend — Thermopylae, Cannae, Hastings, Waterloo, Verdun. But few of them match the bloody fury of the battle of Stalingrad in 1942-1943, when Adolf Hitler hurled a third of a million Germans into combat against the Russians, only to meet defeat and humiliation. At Stalingrad the confident *Fuehrer* lost not only his elite Sixth Army but all hope of pushing the Soviet Union beyond the Urals and winning Europe's breadbasket as well as the Black Sea oil wells. The contest on the Volga's west bank pointed the way to the collapse of the Third Reich.

Vitally strategic Stalingrad was the outlet of the lower Volga region. Unlike Sevastopol, it had no natural defenses, but instead, it sprawled along the west bank of the Volga, the longest river (2,300 miles) and one of the chief waterways of Europe. The target was the home of great tractor and armament plants. Between Stalingrad and the oncoming Germans there was open steppe country, broken only by a few low-lying hills.

The city was the key to Hitler's strategy. He decided that the way to defeat the Russians was to mass troops and equipment for a major drive at one point. His first goal was the Ukraine. A drive into the Caucasus would deprive the Russians of territory in which much of their industry was located and from which they obtained oil, iron, and manganese.

First steps first. From the fall of 1941 to mid-summer 1942 Hitler attempted to finish one remaining task before he would turn on Stalingrad — he would bring the seige of Sevastopol to a successful conclusion. By the first week in July 1942, German troops surged into Voronezh, just east of the Don River. But here they met strong resistance from the Russians, and they shifted their direction south toward Voroshilovgrad. The important objective of Rostov fell on July 28.

Certain of his own military genius, Hitler now divided his offensive into two parts. He moved one part of his forces to the Caucasus and the other in the direction of the Volga at Stalingrad. Capture of this city would be a triumph. Moscow and Leningrad would be isolated, and Russia's last vital oil supply from the Caspian sea route would be cut off. Hitler had it all planned: the Volga River would become the eastern boundary of his enlarged Third Reich and Russia's breadbasket would be in German hands forever — or for at least a thousand years.

For the *Fuehrer* a victory at Stalingrad would be the most stupendous achievement of his life. He had already absorbed a third of Russia, a third of her coal, a third of her chemical industries. One more mighty effort and the Soviet giant with feet of clay would collapse in ignominy. It was just a matter of weeks, he was sure. He moved his headquarters from East Prussia to a spot near Vinnitsa in the Ukraine. He was supremely confident. Had not his Aryan supermen shown their superiority by tramping over the continent of Europe?

The way was prepared for a tremendous victory. For the task the *Fuehrer* assigned General Friedrich von Paulus and 330,000 of his best men. On August 22, 1942, a giant force stood poised just thirty-six miles from the environs of Stalingrad.

In response to Hitler's signal, four hundred tanks, armored troop carriers, and other vehicles dashed forward. The sky was covered with *Stukas* of the *Luftwaffe* flying speedily eastward. The attackers moved ahead swiftly until they could see the skyline of the Russian city at dusk.

That very night Hitler went to the microphones in Berlin and shouted: "We are attacking Stalingrad and we shall take it!" There was no sense of doubt in the *Fuehrer's* words: this was to be another crushing victory.

He had spoken too soon. Inside Stalingrad the Russians simply refused to accept defeat. Workers left their machines and took up arms. Thousands surged to assembly points already arranged.

German long-range guns flattened three-quarters of the city within a day. For the next two months came one of the most amazing battles of World War II or any war. The assault reduced Stalingrad to a graveyard of shattered buildings, crumbling walls, and rotting corpses. Ironically, the destruction helped the Red defense by making the streets impassable. Defenders attacked stalled German tanks in the mountains of rubble and debris. Russian troops, armed with machine guns and knives, crawled through the smashed apartment houses, factories, and courtyards, and fell on the Germans from flanks and rear. There was bloody hand-to-hand fighting not only for every building, but for every room. Gains were measured in yards.

It was unadulterated slaughter. Both sides found it impossible to bury the dead or even count them. Russian General Talensky gave this word-picture:

Our losses were very heavy, indeed. And yet the people who survived acquired a tremendous experience in the technique of house-to-house fighting.

Two or three men of such experience could be worth a whole platoon. They knew every drain pipe, every manhole, every shell-hole and crater in and around their particular building, they knew every brick that could serve as shelter. Among piles of rubble, to which no tank could penetrate, a man would sit there, inside his manhole or crater, or hole in the floor, and looking through his simple periscope, he would turn on his tommy-gun the moment he saw any German within firing distance.

German losses were appalling. Hitler's commanders were bewildered; one of them informed the *Fuehrer:* "Sir, I can work out the exact day on which I shall lose my last man, if the situation is allowed to continue like this." Hitler flashed back his reply: "Are you commanding the Sixth Army, or am I?"

Alexander Werth, an eyewitness, reported: "Stalingrad is still holding out, and the impression is gaining ground that it may well hold. The Germans, it seems, are no longer even trying to capture it at one swoop, but simply to slice it up like a sausage."

The *Fuehrer* was shattered. Soon he was all apologies as he spoke to the Nazi Old Guard: "I wanted to go to the Volga and do so at a particular point. By chance it bears the name of Stalin himself. . . . People say: 'Why don't the troops finish the job more quickly?' Well, the reason is this: I don't want another Verdun. I prefer to do the job with quite small assault groups. Time is of no-consequence at all."

Hitler, now at the tantrum stage, was lying through his teeth. "My God!" said one Stalingrad veteran, "now he talks of 'quite small assault groups.' If only he had been promoted to full corporal!"

The Nazi leader had still another explanation. Russians, he said, refused to fight like normal men. They were just "swamp animals," and it was impossible to guess what such animals would do next. This was very much like General Braddock's complaint — in North America that bemused British general had called on the Indians to "come out of the woods and fight like Englishmen!"

The sensible thing to do was to retreat — even a military amateur would have known that. Hitler's generals begged him either to send reinforcements or allow them to withdraw temporarily. But they did not really know their pigheaded *Fuehrer.* From him came additional outbursts: "Stay and fight! I am not leaving the Volga!" All the shocked underlings could do was to be quiet and accept this display of military lunacy.

A counterattack was not long in coming. On November 19, 1942, the Russians struck back in two spearheads, one from the north and northeast and the other from the southeast. The Russians relied heavily on bayonet attacks, which they knew would terrify the machine-minded enemy. Gradually, a ring of steel was forged around the invading Sixth Army.

The Russians were helped by their fierce winter. Stalingrad lay at the crossroads of two converging climates — the icy Siberian winds from the northeast and the warm Caspian currents from the south. The clash of cold and warm winds left an unpredictable climate, most of it bad.

Soon the Germans were caught in a huge trap, 25 miles wide from east to west, and 12 miles deep from north to south. Nearly 300,000 freezing Germans were being steadily compressed into a smaller and smaller area. Now their munitions and ammunition dwindled. They were reduced to the extremity of eating horses, dogs, and cats. The animal population of Stalingrad vanished.

Paulus saw the necessity of breaking out of the trap. He reported to Hitler:

> Army encircled. Despite heroic resistance . . . high ground is now in Russian hands. Further enemy forces advancing northwards . . . and also in great strength from the west . . . . The Don now frozen and can be crossed. Fuel supplies almost exhausted. Tanks and heavy weapons will then be immobilized, ammunition situation acute, food supplies available for a further six days.

Hitler would not move an inch. "I have considered the situation carefully. My conclusions remain unaltered. The Sixth Army will not be withdrawn. . . . The Sixth Army will stay where it is. Goering has said that he can keep the army supplied by air. I am not leaving the Volga!"

The Nazi superman was almost hysterical. "Send for the corps commander. Tear off his epaulets. Throw him into jail. It's all his fault." From the *Fuehrer* came still another order: "The forces of the Sixth Army encircled at Stalingrad will henceforth be known as the troops of Fortress Stalingrad."

This was supposed to be a promotion for the weary Nazis. The *Fuehrer* was honoring them by calling them the guardians of a besieged castle. "The duty of fortress troops is to withstand sieges. If necessary they will hold out all winter. I shall come to their relief with a Spring offensive."

The *Luftwaffe* virtually disappeared from the skies. At Stalingrad the troops called again and again for air cover, only to be grievously disappointed. One after another the remaining airfields were captured by Russians. Hermann Goering no longer boasted about his invincible airmen.

The weather became even worse than it had been. There were heavy snowfalls and it turned bitterly cold. German troops caught in the Stalingrad pocket found it impossible to dig into the frozen ground. With the appearance of heavy snows, the small petrol supplies were further diminished. Trucks stuck in the snow. It grew colder and colder. Even as Napoleon before him, Hitler was being attacked by the Russian winter.

The terrible situation was described in this letter sent home by a German soldier:

> We're quite alone, without any help from outside. Hitler has left us in the lurch. Whether this letter gets away or not depends on whether we will hold the airfield. We are lying north of the city. The men in my battery already suspect the truth, but they aren't so exactly informed as I am. So this is what the end looks like. . . . No, we are not going to be captured. When Stalingrad falls you will hear and read about it. Then you will know that I will not return.

Hitler, frustrated, sent in more men. On December 12, 1942, a fresh Panzer division tried to relieve the Sixth Army by piercing the ring at the railroad station of Katelnikovo, only 50 miles from Stalingrad. Russian troops under General Rodion Malinovsky hit this relief army and destroyed half its armor. The rest retreated. On January 8, 1943, the Russians presented General Paulus with a ultimatum demanding surrender within 48 hours. Obeying Hitler, Paulus refused. Within a week the Stalingrad pocket was reduced to some 15 miles long and 9 miles deep, and the German garrison was cut to less than 80,000.

The Sixth Army was in desperate shape. General Kurt Seitzler commented:

> For the ordinary soldier fighting [at Stalingrad], each day simply brought a renewed dose of hunger, need, privation, hardship of every sort, bitter cold, loneliness of soul, hopelessness, fear of freezing or starving to death, fear of suffering wounds which in such circumstances could not be tended. . . . It was a nightmare without end. . . .
>
> Supplies to the fighting troops had ceased almost completely. The soldiers lacked food, ammunition, fuel, equipment of every sort. . . . Whole formations melted away. The Sixth Army was consumed as by a fire until all that was left was slag.

How much longer could the slaughter continue? By late January 1943 the Sixth Army was cut to pieces, a shadow of its old self. In the last twenty days of January more than 100,000 Germans were killed in or near Stalingrad. It was a macabre sight as 12,000 ragged and hungry Germans streamed out of the cellars and caves. Paulus and fifteen generals surrendered in the basement of a department store to a twenty-seven-year-old Russian lieutenant. To such ignominious disgrace had fallen the cream of Hitler's supermen. More than 145,000 dead Germans were burned on the spot.

Hitler was furious. Paulus had surrendered without even the gesture of suicide. "I have no respect," he thundered, "for a man who is afraid of suicide and instead accepts captivity." And the troops should have closed ranks and shot themselves with their last bullets. Surrender — never! Far better the Wagnerian Götterdämmerung. To the desperate Germans at Stalingrad this was operatic corn.

Stalingrad was the graveyard of Hitler's aspirations. "It was," said British historian J. W. Wheeler-Bennett, "perhaps the most monumental isolated example in military history of deliberate and wasteful sacrifice of human life." Never before in German history had so great a body of troops come to so humiliating an end. Hitler had not wanted a second Verdun, but in many ways Stalingrad had the same elemental fury, the same blind conflict of wills as that earlier blood bath. A wave of German flesh and blood had smashed against a wall of Russian steel, only to be thrust back, leaving the soil of Russia covered with corpses. The depressed *Fuehrer* ordered four days of mourning for his lost legions.

Most historians regard the battle of Stalingrad as the key turning point of World War II, although others award the palm to the Battle of Britain in 1940 or the invasion of Normandy in 1944. Whatever its place, Stalingrad proved that Hitler was fallible and that his *Wehrmacht* could be beaten. The magnitude of the victory aroused the hopes of the Allies and gave them new confidence in victory.

ATOMIC BOMB DROPPED ON HIROSHIMA, AUGUST 6, 1945

"Our Lord Jesus, have pity on us!"

THE ULTIMATE turning point in history? It may well have been that summer morning of July 16, 1945, when a great cloud of cosmic fire and smoke rose more than eight miles to the stratosphere over the New Mexican desert. This was the atomic version of the old Arabian story about a poor fisherman and a jinni imprisoned in a bottle. From the test came at long last the weapon that gave Japan a shattering reply to Pearl Harbor and put an end to World War II. Man, pygmy though he was, had invaded the sacred precinct of the cosmos.

As always, behind the fact was a long historical preparation. A half century earlier, French physicist Henri Becquerel had observed that a piece of uranium left in his desk drawer caused the blackening of some adjacent photographic plates. The peculiar property of uranium to emit radiation inspired the chief advance of nuclear physics during the last half century. To support the experimental evidence, Max Planck's quantum theory (1900) and Albert Einstein's special theory of relativity (1905) provided formulae to determine the amount of energy released by the atom. By this time physicists began talking about atomic explosions.

The next step was the task of splitting the atom. To accomplish this and turn loose the energy held within the atom's core, Rutherford, Bohr, Chadwick, Lisa Meitner, and other physicists worked tirelessly. One discovery followed another. As early as 1932 Cockcroft and Walton built at Cambridge University an atom smasher, later to be improved by E. O. Lawrence's cyclotron at the University of California. In 1934 Enrico Fermi, an Italian physicist, made experiments in artificial radioactivity caused by neutron bombardment, for which he was awarded the Nobel Prize in 1938. Then Hahn and Strassman, at the Kaiser Wilhelm Institute in Berlin, split the uranium atom.

157

By this time an international race was on to produce an atomic bomb. After Albert Einstein wrote to President Franklin D. Roosevelt about the possibility of producing an atomic bomb, the American President secretly ordered a gigantic project which ultimately expended two billion dollars. On December 2, 1942, scientists at the University of Chicago were able to produce a controlled chain reaction. The critical task of assembling the bomb was entrusted to J. Robert Oppenheimer, who led operations at Los Alamos. It was a race against time – there were indications that German scientists were well on the road to a similar goal.

The Americans won the race. On August 6, 1945, a giant American superfortress flew over Hiroshima, a Japanese city of about 350,000 people, and dropped a bomb with a destructive force of 20,000 tons of TNT. The bomb exploded over more than ten square miles of wooden houses, destroyed over three square miles by blast and then fire. Buildings of reinforced concrete in the center of the city withstood the blast but they were burned out. Half the city was wiped out in raging clouds of dust and smoke.

There are no exact figures, but it is believed that at least 80,000 people lost their lives. Those who were not killed or wounded by the blast gave way to panic and streamed out of the stricken city. It was necessary to wait a month before Hiroshima could be entered and some semblance of order restored. Casualties nearly doubled within a year as persons suffering from radioactivity died.

The destruction was accompanied by the inexplicable and the bizarre. Roads and railway tracks were not affected. After the flash, radiated heat scorched objects at a distance, but missed others. Asphalt road surfaces retained the "shadows" of passersby at the moment of explosion. Most pregnant women within a thousand yards from the center of the explosion had miscarriages. All those directly under the explosion were instantly charred brown or black. This was a modern, streamlined version of Dante's *Inferno*.

What happened at Hiroshima was told by John Hersey in a 30,000-word story, to which the editors of *The New Yorker* devoted their entire issue of August 31, 1946. Hersey reported the experiences of six survivors at the moment when the atomic bomb flashed over Hiroshima. "They still wonder why they lived when so many others died," Hersey commented. The Reverend Mr. Kiyoshi Tanimoto, Methodist pastor, was saved because he was two miles from the center of the explosion, although houses collapsed all about him. Mrs. Hatsuyo Nakamura, a tailor's widow, 1,350 yards from the center of the explosion, "seemed to fly into the next room over the raised sleeping platform, pursued by parts of the house." Dr. Masakayu Fujii, on the porch of his private hospital, 1,550 yards away, was "squeezed tightly by two long timbers in a V across his chest, like a morsel suspended between two huge chop sticks."

Everyday lives immediately dissolved into nightmare. Jesuit Father Wilhelm Kleinsorge, stunned by the flash, found himself wandering around in the mission's vegetable garden in his underwear. His housekeeper kept crying in Japanese, "Our Lord Jesus, have pity on us!" The only physician in the Red Cross hospital to escape injury was Dr. Terufumi Sasaki, surgeon. Soon there began an invasion of his hospital by maimed and dying citizens "that was to make Dr. Sasaki forget his private nightmare for a long, long time." Miss Toshi Sasaki, clerk in a tinworks plant 1,600 yards from the center of the catastrophe, was crushed when her room suddenly collapsed, and her left leg was pinned down by a falling bookcase. "There, in the tin factory, in the first moment of the atomic age, a human being was crushed by books."

In a flash a great city was obscured by a great rolling cloud of smoke and dust. Huge drops of water the size of marbles began to fall — condensed moisture falling from the tower of dust, heat, and fission fragments miles above stricken Hiroshima. Streets were littered with parts of houses that had collapsed and sheets of flame whipped crazily through the city. The eyebrows of some victims were burned off and skin hung from their faces and hands. Others, because of pain, held their arms as if carrying something in both hands. Some were vomiting as they walked. There was a strong odor of ionization, an electric smell given off by the bomb's fission. When the dust settled, an area of three square miles was leveled except for a few reinforced concrete walls.

The Japanese were terrorized by the destructive power of the first atomic bomb on Hiroshima, as well as the second on Nagasaki three days later. Emperor Hirohito, disregarding the advice of fanatical patriots, sued for peace. The war quickly came to an end. The instrument of surrender was signed in Tokyo Bay aboard the battleship *Missouri* on September 2, 1945.

Within five years after the disaster, Hiroshima was rebuilt, with wide roads, parks, and tree-lined boulevards. Plans were made to make the city a permanent center for culture and peace.

The use of the atomic bomb made it certain that the world would never be the same. The tenor of war was changed   all other weapons were outdated by this revolutionary development. With it came a host of questions. What would happen if in the future this weapon came into the hands of a madman who would use it regardless of consequences? Was it not possible for a relatively small nation to produce the atomic bomb and utilize it for international blackmail?

These and a host of related questions rose out of the quagmire of confusion surrounding atomic energy. Intelligent men were worried that the inquiring mind had led humanity to the brink of destruction. With improved versions of the new weapon it was entirely possible to burn the earth to ashes. Before his death the genius Oppenheimer became a tortured soul, appalled by the power of the weapon he had helped create.

At the present moment the atomic bomb maintains the peace on a balance-by-terror basis. Perhaps it might shock the human animal into putting an end to his perverse sense of nationalism and encourage him to live in peace with his neighbors. If so, atomic energy might turn out to be a tremendous force for good. If not, the long process of evolution will lead straight to oblivion with life on this planet as extinct as the dinosaur, and the surrounding atmosphere contaminated by radioactivity. There would then be no need for further turning points in the story of man's sojourn on this planet.